Like Gold Through Fire

"This is a profound and moving book that confronts human suffering, perhaps the most difficult aspect of our lives, with honesty, deep wisdom, and compassion. The authors look for no easy answers; rather, they undertake a courageous and unflinching journey into this deep mystery of life. Seldom since Carl Jung hi[illegible]self have any authors undertaken such an important and [illegible] [illegible]bject from a perspective that combines religion a[illegible] [illegible]similla and Bud Harris draw on Chris[illegible] [illegible] to grapple helpfully with the terrible a[illegible] [illegible]uffering."

—[illegible]key, Ph.D.
[illegible]disciplinary Studies
[illegible]ppalachian State University

"This book is a blessing! Massimilla and Bud Harris have created a brilliant synthesis of theology, Jungian psychology, and philosophy as a guide through the darkness of suffering's descent and into transformation's emerging glory. The text builds and deepens with strength, calling the reader to faithfulness in the individuation process where our wounds become the agents to break open our hearts so that what is needed for life's wholeness may flow in. I keep this book close at hand in my work as a psychotherapist and as one learning to dance with chronic illness."

—*Les Rhodes, M.A., AAMFT, CFLE Psychotherapist*

"This is not an easy book to read, not because of complicated ideas or language, but because with clarity and profundity, it drives its point straight into the heart and changes forever the me who reads it. This is a book to experience, not to understand. It brings whatever life experience, religious experience, and psychological experience one has together in such a way that the reading itself is transformative."

"Of particular interest to me was the weaving together of Jungian psychology and the life of Jesus. This was accomplished—not by explaining the mysteries surrounding Christ, his suffering, the cross, and the connection between mother and spirit—but by illuminating them with a light that we can see into and feel into the heart, and with that seeing and feeling calls the reader to go deeper into the mystery and, thus, deeper into life itself."

—*Judith C. Boyd, Ph.D..,* Psychotherapist

"A book to heal so many wounds of misunderstood suffering. Suffering not as blame or God's punishment, suffering not seen as mysteriously meaningful per se. Suffering as the painful transformation into someone's innermost truth. And only then to be seen as part of the process where the suffering God and suffering men and women break through all mankind's traumata of murder and despair. Till then we often have only that paradoxical word: 'Blessed are the sorrowful; they shall find consolation.'"

—*Dirk Evers,, Ph.D.* Training Analyst,
Jung Institute, Zurich

"Filled with warmth, human compassion, and hope, this book presents a deep and uplifting view of human suffering. It gives up the necessary wisdom that weaves our daily experiences and our deep agonies into a dance of transformation, joy, and wholeness."

—*Linda A. van Dyck, Jungian Analyst*

"What the Harrises have achieved in *Like Gold Through Fire: Understanding the Transforming Power of Suffering* is to imagine forward and articulate C. G. Jung's original assertion that neurosis is not always just a repressed conflict, but is sometimes a "false" solution to one of life's tasks that the neurotic is not living up to. By differentiating the aspects of suffering beyond *natural*, *developmental* and *neurotic* suffering, [the Harrises have designated] a higher level of consciousness [of] the *transcendent* mode of suffering, which connects us to the transpersonal realm of life and the deeper center of our personality that Jung called the 'Self.' The point of this approach is to go into the 'point of the suffering' in order to gain a broader understanding of its place in our lives and to then be prepared to move into a 'higher (or deeper) and more authentic level' of living."

—*Battle Bell,* Jungian Analyst

"The profound depth of these two analysts shines through in *Like Gold Through Fire*. Using myth, fairy tale, religion, and real-life experiences, the authors weave a penetrating imagination of the role of suffering in our lives. The work encourages us to have a conscious relationship to our own suffering so that real compassion and joy can be born. As a psychotherapist and teacher, the insights found in this work have added meaning and substance to my work."

—*Janet S. Hampton, M.S.,* Psychotherapist

LIKE
GOLD
THROUGH FIRE

LIKE GOLD THROUGH FIRE

A Message in Suffering

A Guide for Understanding the Psychology of Suffering and Transformation

by

Massimilla M. Harris

and

Bud Harris

ALEXANDER BOOKS
65 Macedonia Road
Alexander, North Carolina 28701

Publisher: Ralph Roberts
Vice-President/Operations: Pat Hutchison Roberts

Editors: Ralph Roberts, Pat Hutchison Roberts, Gayle Graham

Cover design: Mark Wilson and **WorldComm**®
Cover and interior art: Tom Schulz
Cover photograph: Livio Piatti
Interior design & electronic Page Assembly: **WorldComm**®
Indexing: The Roberts Group

Printed in the United States of America.

10 9 8 7 6 5 4 3 2 1

Library of Congress Cataloging-in-Publication

Harris, Massimilla M., 1949—
Like gold through fire : a message in suffering : a guide for understanding the psychology of suffering and transformation / Massimilla M. Harris and Bud Harris.
p. cm.
Includes bibliographical references and index
ISBN 1-57090-020-5 (alk. paper)
1. Suffering--Religious aspects--Christianity. 2. Suffering. 3. Jungian psychology. 4. Psychoanalysis and religion. I. Harris, Bud, 1937— . II. Title.
BV4909.H37 1996
231'.8--dc20 96-15762
CIP

The opinions expressed in this book are solely those of the author and are not necessarily those of Alexander Books.

Alexander Books—a division of Creativity, Inc.—is a full–service publisher located at 65 Macedonia Road, Alexander NC 28701. Phone (704) 252–9515, Fax (704) 255–8719. For orders only: 1-800-472-0438. Visa and MasterCard accepted.

Alexander Books is distributed to the trade by Midpoint Trade Books, Inc., 27 West 20th Street, New York NY 10011, (212) 727-0190, (212) 727-0195 fax.

Acknowledgments

Every effort has been made to trace all copyright holders but if any has been inadvertently overlooked, the author and publisher will be pleased to make the necessary arrangement at the first opportunity.

Crucifixion, S. Maria Antiqua, p. 105 © Alinari/Art Resources, NY
Crucifix, Giunta Pisano, p. 107 ©Scala/Art Resources, NY
The Crucifixion, Mt.. Sinai, p. 109, from David Talbot Rice, A Concise History of Painting from Prehistory to the Thirteenth Century (New York: Frederick A. Praeger, 1968, Figure 78).
Christ on the Tree of Life and The Cross on Adam's Grave, p 109, from C. G. Jung, Symbols of Transformation, Collected Works (Princeton, NJ. : Princeton University Press, 1956, figures 36 and 37).
The Crucifixion, Salador Dali, p. 114 ©The Metropolitan Museum of Art, Gift of The Chester Dale Collection, 1955.
Excerpt from C. S. Lewis, The Great Divorce (New Your: Macmillon, 1946, pp. 98-103) reprinted by permission of Harper Collins Publishers Ltd.
Excerpt from C. S. Jung, Letters, vols. I and II (London: Routledge and Kegan, 1976, p. 236 and pp. 492-493) reprinted by permission of the publisher.
Excerpts from C. G. Jung, Man and His Symbols (New York: Doubleday, 1964, p. 82) reprinted by permission of J. C. Ferguson Publishing.
Excerpt from C. G. Jung, Memories, Dreams, Reflections (New York: Pantheon, 109773. p. 277) reprinted by permission of the publisher.
Excerpts from C. G. Jung, Collected Works (Princton, NJ. :Princeton University Press) reprinted by permission of the publisher.
Excerpts from Sheldon B. Kopp, If You Meet Buddha on the Road Kill Him (Palo Alto, Calif.: Science and Behavior Books, Inc., 1972) reprinted by permission of the author and the publisher.
Excerpt from Fratz Zorn, Mars, Robert and Rita Kimber, Trans. © 1981 by Alfred A. Knopt, Inc. Reprinted by permission of the publisher.
Excerpt from the Complete Grimm's Fairy Tales by Jakob Ludwig and Wilhelm Karl Grimm, trans. by James Stern © 1944 by Pantheon Books, Inc., and renewed 1972 by Random House, Inc. Reprinted by permission of Pantheon Books, a division of Random House, Inc.

PREFACE

One of the sure signs that you've reached a turning point in your life is that existence seems barren and at an impasse. You lose your vision, you can't find your path, you're tormented by warring thoughts, and you wonder if you'll ever be happy again. Endurance feels like being on a painful psychic cross. The pain is compounded because we live in a world oriented toward more and more pleasure and dedicated to the denial and avoidance of pain. At the same time, our world leaves us feeling abandoned and lonely, leading to a myriad of addictions and a high crime and suicide rate, especially among our young. The fact of the matter is that life has become so complicated and so alienated that we no longer know what "goodness" or "happiness" really means. But those of us in the therapeutic community are deluged with people who "only want to be happy" or "only want their children to be happy."

Modern society has trained us to see dark times as weakness or pathology, and because of this we have forgotten that these periods may begin the great transformative experiences that become the mother of human destiny. All great religions were born in conflict and suffering, yet our consumer-oriented religious institutions have de-emphasized the passion and crucifixion in order to accent the "Good News." We are taught to believe that if our religion is outside of us, invested in some organization or doctrine, instead of within our own hearts, then we should not have to suffer. In modern Christianity, an institutional Christ has done it for us, suffered for our sins, whatever you might imagine sin to be. Or someone else such as the Lamed Vovniks, the Just Men of the Hebrew tradition, will be open to carrying the suffering of the world. Not one of the great mystics in any religion would accept this interpretation of spirituality.

In trying to avoid suffering, we have lost touch with the great spiritual and psychological process: *life, death, decay* and *renewal,* where every step is ushered in or out by suffering. Vitality, joy, suffering, and meaning, which used to go hand in hand in the ancient rituals and great spiritual traditions, are now considered incompatible opposites.

Religion, psychology, and philosophy unite to tell us that we must know who we are and what we are doing in this journey we call life. And we must recognize once again that each new level of consciousness, each new level of personal and societal development, is won through conflict and suffering. Every time our life energy returns to our inner being to prepare for a renewal or to deal with an obstacle to our growth, we experience it as a depression– and we need to know the meanings behind these processes. Our purpose in exploring suffering is to help us take part again in the process of life, to know when to surrender to the stream of life, the unknown, that can transform us and carry us to healing, wisdom, and a destiny beyond our comprehension. Only in this fashion can we begin to find ourselves at home in ourselves and in a world that reaches beyond the frantic, nervous, soul-destroying surface reality of modern life.

Many of the Christian mystics consider that eternal life, the major theme of Saint John's gospel, begins with a fuller, richer, freer life in this world. Such a life is found through a more authentic relationship with God as the center of one's self and leads to a life lived more authentically as a person rather than as a pseudo-person living by others' expectations. Jungian psychology follows a similar vein, noting that we come to feel at home in ourselves as we differentiate ourselves from the expectations of others and learn to follow the deeper voice coming from the center of our being. Then we are able to relate to others more authentically, contribute personally to culture, and live out the destiny inherent in our personality.

We would like to make a couple of comments on how this book

is written. We write as Jungian analysts, but we are also religious people, and many of our terms, comments, and traditional images are theological. This should not be surprising since the great questions of life are addressed in philosophy, religion, and psychology. In our search for understanding, we may have to differentiate between these fields, but they are all rooted in our psyche and, at some point, must come home together. So although psychology and religion are separate for the most part in their institutional forms, we are comfortable working in both camps at once. Whatever separation you think is necessary, we leave up to you.

We also struggled with the question of whether this book should be a presentation for readers who are suffering or for the professionals who counsel them. In the end, we decided that, once again, this issue is a false dichotomy. The best professionals (whether in psychology or religion) are those who have suffered, are still suffering, and are aware of it. This presentation is intended for those interested in embracing what it means to be human. Our purpose is not to *give* you answers, but to *aid* in the forging of your own answers.

Finally, the dreams and case histories presented in this book are intended for illustrative purposes. We have disguised the personal information and, at times, made composites of many case experiences. The resulting illustrations represent real-life experiences while obscuring the identity of any one person. Any similarity between these illustrations and an actual individual is purely coincidental.

CONTENTS

Without suffering, happiness cannot be understood. The ideal passes through suffering like gold through fire.

–Fyodor Dostoevski

Foreword to: A Message In Suffering

by Robert Sardello, Ph.D.

In our age, a false flight from suffering, nurtured by the strictly modern fantasy that medicine, counseling, a support group, or community service can remove it is simultaneously paired with more visible suffering in the world than perhaps has ever been seen before. To convey, as the Harrises have done in this bold work, that suffering in fact gives us the most direct means of coming to terms with the mystery of our being, with what makes us human, may seem at the very least, masochistic. Should we not do all in our power to alleviate suffering–our own and that of others? Of course, we not only should, we must. But, there are two ways, two attitudes that can be taken toward alleviating suffering–a mechanical, technical, materialistic way and a soul and spiritual way.

The modern way responds to pain by using the wonders of modern technology, whether that takes the form of instruments and scientific discovery, or the technology of transporting food, clothing, and medicines to disaster victims within a few hours, or economic technology of getting money to where it is needed. Indeed, those of us who value soul do so from the perspective of a world having the means and the will to do something about suffering; only the naive would set up technology as in opposition to soul. A soul perspective, however, does try to bring balance–balance by drawing attention to the inescapable fact that suffering is a tremendously important teacher; balance by trying to help us see that technology does not, in fact, remove suffering (at most it makes possible the alleviation of natural suffering, so that, in the Harrises' terms, developmental and transcendent suffering may take place with proper timing); balance in the sense of helping to distinguish between neurotic and transcendent suffering so that suffering is allowed its meaning rather than being repetitious self-indulgence masquerading as agony. The first reality that this book asks us to confront, and to ponder deeply, is that suffering, finally, cannot be denied, displaced, avoided, or projected, nor, ultimately, gotten rid of.

Suffering without consciousness differs enormously from suffering that has found its proper mode of consciousness. In the extreme case, suffering without consciousness is simply denial. Louise Lavelle, a truly great writer on the problem of evil and suffering, said that the worst misery is not to be aware of misery. Then there is suffering that, while strongly felt, still has no psychic element–it simply hurts and all of the psychic element is placed into the fantasy of escape, where it has no value. The many stories, fairy tales, myths, and personal case histories told by the Harrises give us an indication of the direction where suffering does locate its own meaning–the direction is down, into the depths, like the underworld terrain of Inanna, or of Persephone, where the true psychic element of suffering is to be found. This terrain is difficult to speak of other than in imaginal terms.

As soon as the word "imagination" arises there is a tendency to discount it as real. My suffering, that is real; the imaginal, well that is the making of nice or not so nice stories, but they are only stories. The reader might react in this fashion. What these imaginal pictures convey, however, is value. These imaginal pictures, note well, are not saying that there is value in suffering but that suffering is the very source of value. In the absence of recognizing that to suffer means to allow something to happen to us that we cannot control, we have no importance, no merit, value, substance, purpose as human beings. We reach the realm of value only by allying our very being with the reality of suffering. Only imaginal pictures can convey this fact without false sentiment. Concentrating, contemplating, meditating on the many stories in this book, reading them through over and over, making inner pictures, not skimming, looking for answers, this marvelous work truly does turn into a guide book, a path into the depths that has no bottom.

How does one enter rightly into the realm where suffering shows it true continence as the source of value? This question is also addressed by the Harrises, but I want to bring it out, perhaps letting it sound more clearly. There is a science of suffering, and that science is patience. Indeed, suffering often turns us into a patient. The word patience suggests passivity, a kind of waiting without stirring and without hope; to be still, so that something else can awaken. What awakens is soul life; and it does so in every cell of the body. Even more, what awakens is the deepest and the highest dimension of soul life, the divine within us. Jungians call this the Self, but the term can get in the way of sensing the actual experience of being touched by the presence of the divine. I suspect that people are so belligerently reluctant to relinquish neurotic suffering, because it gives them a sense, albeit a false sense, of the near presence of the divine. The science and art of patience involves developing the capacity to wait, in an attitude of expectation while at the same time having relinquished the expectation that something will happen. This mystery, too, we are confronted with in this book.

Suffering, when it does receive a nod of recognition as valuable, receives its acknowledgment from pairing it with transformation. Yes, there is Good Friday and hanging on the cross; but then there is Easter Sunday and the Resurrection. Yes, there is the bitterness of winter, but then that makes possible the spring. Transformation is a most tricky word, almost as tricky as the word "healing," but not as tricky as the word "salvation." So, let us face it head on. Transformation means death. None of us know, as far as our individual lives are concerned, what is on the other side, discounting of course, the initiates and the true sufferers among the readers. We need others; we need the Buddhist and the Yoga philosophies, the Christian mystics, and the psychic initiates such as Jung to show us pictures, to provide imagination where we have none. Evoking transformation as the reason for human suffering can too easily slide into a kind of egotism–hey, this is worth doing, look where it gets me. Fortunately, the Harrises do not fall into this trap. They are too good of analysts for this; they recognize the difference between theory and what can be validated through one's own experience. They say: "In dealing with suffering, analysts to some extent share the same professional field as psychologists and doctors. However, our approach differs in that we not only study the theories of psychology, but also experience their validity within our own personal lives as we train" (pg.123). That is to say, only those who suffer have the right to say anything about the mystery of suffering.

The word "transformation" takes on quite a different quality when spoken from having encountered it deeply. If I read of suffering, and unwittingly read only from ego consciousness, there is no other possibility than literalizing the word and taking it to mean that transformation means the way out, even if it is a more complex way than a pain pill. Read from the perspective of the Harrises' life work, transformation is not the way out at all, but the deepening of the way into it. And this deepening consists of transforming into a religious being–not simply one who believes, who has faith, who listens to the preacher–there is nothing religious in that. But, being a religious being, in every fiber of one's body, every feeling of one's soul, every thought, every action, through and through, that is transformation. And, truly, there are no words for this; thus we need pictures and we need these pictures brought by those who live in wisdom.

The purpose of speaking so deeply of suffering, as the authors of this book do, is not only to help us fathom the depths of this mystery in the privacy of our own hearts. Suffering, even if entered into with soul, remains untransformed so long as it remains private. Here, I want to touch upon something not explicitly spoken of in this book. Yet, this book, by its very existence, circulating in the world, is testimony to the fact that suffering finds its true meaning only when it is shared. Following the wonderful exemplar of this book, perhaps a good way to approach this most significant dimension of suffering is through a story. Sophocles gives us such a story, *Philoctetes.*

Philoctetes, on the way to Troy with Agamemnon and Menelaus, got off the ship at the tiny island of Chryse to sacrifice to the local gods. As he was walking up to the shrine, he was bitten on the foot by a viper, a bite that immediately became infected. Black and festering, it was soon a raging, bleeding sore. Pus and rot attracted maggots to the wound, filling the air with a stench that no man could stomach. His companions, nauseous from the sight and smell of the wound, took him from Chryse and left him on a deserted island, Lemnos. There was nothing on that island–no trees, no plants, no animals–only dry earth and rock crags. Philoctetes would not have survived except for the bow and arrow given to him by Heracles. Heracles had received that bow from Apollo himself and had given it to Philoctetes when he was dying; for Philoctetes had served him by lighting his funeral pyre. It was a remarkable instrument, that bow. It never missed the mark, such was its precision. Though few were the birds flying overhead, he never missed a shot and life was thus barely possible.

For ten years all there was on that island of suffering was Philoctetes, his maggot-ridden, never-healing foot, and a dead bird to eat from time to time. Filled with bitterness and rage, isolated and lonely, Philoctetes gave up on humankind and gods alike: "In all I saw before me nothing but pain; but of that a great abundance." Then one day a ship comes to the shore. Two figures leave and step onto the island. One of them is Odysseus, and the other, a young man, Neoptolemus, son of Achilles. They came to retrieve Philoctetes, for an oracle said that Troy could be conquered only with the help of Philoctetes and his bow. The plan is to trick him into coming with them. When Neoptolemus meets and talks with Philoctetes, he finds he cannot trick him. He admires the courage he sees; he waits with Philoctetes, hears his stories, cares for him. Odysseus, watching from afar, finally enters, and threatens to force Philoctetes to leave. Philoctetes grabs his bow and is about to shoot Odysseus when suddenly Heracles appears in a vision, telling Philoctetes that he must go to Troy. There he will recover health and obtain glory.

On the island, Philoctetes festers in bitterness and rage, turning against the gods and all humans for this bitter injustice. He says to himself: "Necessity has taught me little by little to suffer and be patient." Being patient, paradoxically, means, as I suggested above, forgetting one's connections–with others, with the gods, with hope itself. And, in suffering, one is removed from the community of others; suffering is the only reality. No one is there to say what is happening, why it is happening, what brought it, where it is going.

When we are suffering, the explanations, the happy prognoses, the encouragement of those around seem hollow and unreal. The name, Philoctetes, means "love of possessions." I do not know if this individual had many possessions, but now he is not even in possession of himself. He no longer belongs to himself; he belongs to suffering. The bow and arrow, instruments of bare survival, are like a terminal cancer patient connected to life support. Like this magical bow, modern, technical instrumentation does not take suffering away, but it does make survival possible.

Heracles gives Philoctetes the bow. Heracles also appears in the vision and tells Philoctetes to leave the island. Heracles, the hero, brings imagination to suffering. Andre Gide's modern version of this Greek drama illustrates this aspect clearly. Gide's Philoctetes states:

"My images, since I have been alone, so that nothing, not even suffering, disturbs them, have taken a subtle course which sometimes I can hardly follow. I have come to know more of the secrets of life than my masters had ever revealed to me. And I took to telling stories of my sufferings ...I came to understand that words inevitably become more beautiful from the moment they are no longer put together in response to the demands of others."

Here, we see that through suffering imagination comes to prominence. Without imagination, suffering is blind necessity. But imagination has to come to us; it is not something done solely out of our own efforts. And, imagination brings something new to speech. It makes possible moving into the imaginal fabric of words themselves rather than just wing words to convey something to others. Said in another way, truth comes to expression; imagination no longer belongs to the realm of the unconscious.

Heracles is evidently no ordinary hero. He is the only Greek hero who at the moment of his death becomes a god, becomes a figure of the eternal archetypal realm of the soul. Thus, he appears in a vision–and he encourages Philoctetes to return to the human community. But, we have to see that this moment of intervention occurs primarily because of the presence of Neoptolemus. Odysseus remains in the background. But Neoptolemus, while he does not seem to do much, certainly nothing heroic, laments, mourns, and cries out with the suffering of this individual. Philoctetes says, "You stayed with me; you had pity, looked after me, bore with the filthy disease." That is all Neoptolemus does. But this consolation creates a new community, lets suffering have a part in the communal imagination.

We mistakenly suppose that the instruments of survival have the power to take away suffering. But those who have suffered deeply know that it does not go away, ever. While, in some quarters of Jungian thought, the hero is identified as our ego consciousness and entering into soul is a necessary and deadly blow to the ego, the true hero was never simply someone with an inflated ego. The true hero, one who suffers, discovers something there that is brought back to the community, for the benefit of the whole community. This book is such a Heraclean work. And it is also the consolation of Neoptolemus, making possible a community of suffering

Something of the ultimate secret of suffering is revealed in an almost passing sentence of this book The authors say: "As we go through the individuation process and our suffering transforms from developmental or neurotic into transcendent, we find that more and more it is the divine aspect in us that suffers" (pg. 149). A remarkable sentence that brings a flood of thoughts. Can we imagine that God is a suffering God? More, that the very essence of the divine is suffering? But, a contradicting thought says, God is love, not suffering. Ah, but here we can get a glimpse through the veil of the constantly sentimentalized word, love. Everyone knows, whether they dare to speak it or not, that love is suffering. Of course, there is neurotic love, every bit as much as there is neurotic suffering. But, if we have come as far in the contemplation of this book to awaken to the fact of the sacred nature of suffering, then we have to at least say we are brought to the very edge of love itself.

The position that suffering is love is taken by Jung in his most astounding work, *Answer to Job.* I will not here go into this complex book. It is a guiding model for the process of making suffering meaningful. Suffice it to say that Jung proposes that God needs human beings in order to become conscious, that God is evolving and needs human beings in order to evolve, and the primary way through which God becomes conscious is through human suffering. The individuation process is the human contribution to divine self-realization. What could God possibly be unaware of? He is not conscious of his other half, the feminine being of Sophia. When we have entered so deeply into suffering that there we discover something that is impossible to describe in words–that there in the very center of suffering dwells the divine being of Sophia, we have found the ultimate meaning of suffering as love. For, once Sophia, Wisdom, the Pietà, the Mater Dolorosa, the Soul of the World is encountered, a path is established for reconnection with Her Beloved. Only Jung's psychology gives us the direction, the means, and the courage for treading this sacred path of suffering. The Harrises, in this marvelous book, help us to begin this holy work.

–Robert Sardello, Ph.D.

Author of
Facing the World with Soul
and *Love and the Soul*

1

Introduction: Pain, Suffering, Transformation, and Joy

Words, like the stories they compose, often reflect the obsessions and blind spots of the cultures that create them. The word "suffering" has degenerated in our age to mean almost any kind of physical or emotional discomfort. It is a synonym for depression, affliction, despair, hopelessness, and grief. All of these terms suggest a weight bearing *down*, or of a person being struck down in some way. Our modern concept of suffering means being brought low.

Because of this perspective, we find *suffering*, as a concept, a difficult idea to pursue, to consider, and to meditate upon. We would prefer to push it into the background of our lives, and hope that fate never brings it into the foreground. But fate follows its own course, and history, as well as psychology and religion, teaches us that the seeds of transformation and new life generally reside in the areas we have rejected and secretly fear. With this paradox in mind, let's begin to consider the word *suffering*.

In Latin, *sufferentiam* means "patience," and the verb "sufferre" is formed by combining "sub" and "ferre." Literally, this combination means to "carry up from under." Helen Luke[1] suggests that this meaning reminds her of "the term undercarriage–that which bears the weight of a vehicle above the wheels–which is an apt image of the meaning of suffering in human life."

Another common image for suffering in folklore[2] is that of an old woman carrying a heavy stone on her shoulders. In order to manage this, we might imagine that she has to bend a little to distribute the weight so she doesn't lose her balance. She also has to know where to go, where to step, in order to conserve her energy and to move without the risk of falling. Finally, she has to watch carefully where she puts each foot one step at a time while concentrating on the ground in front of her rather than the landscape around her. With a little imagination this simple image from folklore turns into an allegory for dealing with suffering.

However, what commonly happens is that we simply lie down under the weight of our miseries or deny them and don't move at all. We refuse to pick up our burden–whether circumstance, mood, or both–and therefore, try to avoid the experience of real suffering.

More often than we like to admit, we have made our burdens into secret friends and may even use them to rescue us from the difficult decisions and circumstances we are facing. Frequently, it seems more convenient to simply accept our aching luggage because it is the "right" thing to do. But in the long run, it is better to look for a deeper understanding of our suffering. This perspective will mean taking on the hard inner work of confronting our illusions of who we are and the false humility and pride we have developed around our self-image. But in the end, if we can bear a tiny portion, our portion, of the struggle with the darkness of the world, we can participate in the important work of bringing meaning into our lives. Then we begin to release our personal concerns and take part in a process of life bigger than ourselves.

Evelyn Underhill calls this wider process *Reality*,[3] which includes the "material for a more intense life, a wider, sharper consciousness, a more profound understanding." Underhill speaks of the reality of the mystics, the unity with a higher spiritual plane, the deeper REALITY that supports everyday life with eternal values and meaning and that offers us a true sense of being at home in life.

Facing our sorrows honestly also will enable us to go beyond the experience of personal emotions and participate in the sorrows of others, in compassion. The etymological meaning of the word compassion is "with suffering" or "suffering with." Through this process we can learn more about life and develop more sensitivity, strength, and a closer and more vital relationship with ourselves and our neighbors.

The first step in finding a deeper understanding of suffering is to recognize and fight the tendency in our culture to deny it. Suffering has become meaningless to us. We regard it as something to be avoided, something extraneous, something to be cured. A person who is suffering is someone to be pitied, someone who is unfortunate if not outright pathological. Modern parents show this tendency to resist suffering when they are more concerned for their children's future security and happiness than the development of their character and destiny.

We try to believe it is possible to forget about sad things, and focus on pleasant comforts and activities. We think that we should be able to put it behind us and get on with our lives. By striving for such an attitude, we reduce suffering to an *inferior* role in our experience. This reduction unbalances our psychological ecology, the primary system of life encompassing the union, balance, and interaction of opposites.

Carl Jung recognized the need of suffering for psychological health when he wrote:

> "The principal aim of psychotherapy is not to transport the patient to an impossible state of happiness, but to help him acquire steadfastness and philosophic patience in face of suffering. Life demands for its completion and fulfillment a balance between joy and sorrow. But because suffering is positively disagreeable, people naturally prefer not to ponder how much fear and sorrow fall to the lot of man. So they speak soothingly about progress and the greatest possible happiness, forgetting that happiness is itself poisoned if the measure of suffering has not been fulfilled. Behind a neurosis there is so often concealed all the natural and necessary suffering the patient has been unwilling to bear."[4]

Classifications of Suffering

No matter how developed modern civilized people might

appear, they still harbor an archaic man or woman in the deeper layers of their psyche. Archaic humanity, according to Lévy-Bruhl, lived in a state of "participation mystique," maintaining an unconscious harmony with events in both the inner and outer world and forming a coherent whole with them. Anything psychological was projected[5] on the outside world, and there was no difference between the various kinds of suffering because all suffering came from offending the gods. Primitives performed rituals and offered sacrifices to the Supreme Being, or the priest or sorcerer, with his amulets, potions, or weapons, tried to win the favor of the gods or spirits. In this way they made their suffering understandable and were able to tolerate it.

As we become more conscious, we start to separate inner and outer reality. We also begin to discriminate between different kinds of suffering. Some kinds (say, breaking a leg at a softball game) are more or less immediate, and others (say, grief over a lost love) are more or less profound. "Profound" is another word that bears further investigation. It comes from the Latin words meaning to come from great depths and means thoroughgoing and far-reaching, penetrating beyond what is superficial or obvious.[6] It also means absolute and complete. Profound suffering, as we define it, can be the road to the deeper Reality of the mystics, the unity of life that transcends the two modes of consciousness, inner and outer, and unity with this Reality is not an easy stage to reach, as Evelyn Underhill points out in her books on mysticism. This unity is not the passive or transcendent delight of the so-called new age. The path of classical mysticism is through self-discipline and suffering, the suffering of the opposites–being willing to struggle with the ambivalent nature of life and the ambivalences within our own nature. But this profound suffering is often misunderstood, and we must distinguish it from more superficial forms of suffering.

Natural disasters, diseases, or the death of a loved one bring us face to face with a fundamental type of suffering that is closely connected with the cycle of life and death. Such suffering is instinctive, innate, and also inevitable. We might call it *natural* suffering, since it reflects the ongoing process of nature. Understanding this cycle of life and death and accepting its totality consciously is a lifetime task–part of what in Jungian terms is called the "Individuation Process."[7]

The individuation process also gives rise to another kind of suffering that we call *developmental* suffering. This suffering is natural in the sense that it is part of the normal process of development, but it is distinct from natural suffering in that it is driven from within us, even though it might be triggered from without.

This awareness is the beginning step in developing what depth psychology calls an "ego" (from the Latin for "I"), or what we more generally call a personality. Our ego is the organizing center of our conscious mind, the seat of our identity and the reference point for our experiences. And to a large extent it develops by adapting to the circumstances in which we are born.

The developmental path of the ego is not an easy one. As our ego adapts to life, we choose preferred ways of relating to the world, gathering information, and making decisions. These preferences combine with our temperament to give us a sense of identity that remains roughly constant both to ourselves and others. But the identity that grows also reflects our wounds–springing from parents and other environmental factors who were either cold, uncaring, smothering, frightening, or so on–as well as our strengths and can limit us as well as support us. So as we grow and become more conscious of ourselves, we must face the limits we have incorporated in our identity if we are to deal with them and so lead a more authentic life. Facing our limitations often involves a lot of developmental suffering.

The developing ego may be likened to a seed planted in the earth that sprouts toward the light and sometimes finds itself blocked by a stone in its path. The young plant has to grow around the stone before it can reach the light, so that its final shape is often very different from what it could have been. Then, as the plant matures, it must learn to produce fruit the best that it can, given the soil it was planted in.

Sometimes the rocks can be so big or the soil so lacking in nutrients and water that the seed never breaks out into the light. In extreme cases, an ego may even turn back on itself. When a person with such an undeveloped ego faces the decisions, tasks, and impasses that are often a part of natural suffering, they develop an inner split in their personalities. They may begin seeking refuge in the past or the future, in compulsive rituals or in some illusion, because their here and now is unbearable. They may even develop several completely distinct personalities. These inner splits in the ego make up a third type of suffering: *neurotic* suffering.

Neurotic suffering arises from a conflict between the longing for growth and freedom on the one hand and the inability or refusal to pay the required price in developmental suffering on the other.

Beyond *natural*, *developmental* and *neurotic* suffering, there is at a higher level of consciousness a *transcendent* mode of suffering, which connects us to the transpersonal realm of life and the deeper center of our personality that Jung called the "Self." At this level, the language of psychology becomes notably similar to the language of prayer. When our ego has developed a capacity to go beyond its own wants and fulfillments and serve the cause of the Self, it has done so not only in spite of, but also because of unavoidable suffering. For example, when we are faced with an *impossible* situation, we may have to accept the transcendent suffering involved in changing ourselves and, paradoxically, this action changes the outer situation. Gandhi, Martin Luther King, and Mother Theresa of Calcutta all illustrate the conscious and powerful use of this actuality.

The Self, as Jung understood it, represents both the center and the totality of our personality. It is the sun in the solar system supplying the energy of life; it is the earth supporting and nurturing all growth. As the totality of our personality, it combines in potential all of our mental processes and characteristics, positive and negative, in their full range from constructive to destructive. But these contents don't exist in chaos, they are parts of the pattern of development for our whole person. Because the Self is greater than our personal sense of identity, being in touch with it is a transcendent experience. For the same reason, the Self is often considered the image of God within each of us.

In order to reach this transcendent suffering, we must undergo developmental suffering, even if it means becoming aware of and then transforming neurotic suffering. Paradoxically, the process requires both active seeking and passive receptivity, two processes often combined in analysis as well as in many spiritual exercises.

Facing Neurotic Suffering—*The Great Divorce*

The following story by C.S. Lewis[8] beautifully illustrates the psychic push and pull, the desire for and the fear of transformation.

> I saw coming towards us a Ghost who carried something on his shoulder. Like all the Ghosts, he was unsubstantial, but they differed from one another as smokes differ. Some had been whitish; this one was dark and oily. What sat on his shoulder was a little red lizard, and it was twitching its tail like a whip and whispering things in his ear. As we caught sight of him he turned his head to the reptile with a snarl of impatience. "Shut up, I tell you!" he said. It wagged its tail and continued to whisper to him. He ceased snarling, and presently began to smile. Then he turned and started to limp westward, away from the mountains.
>
> "Off so soon?" said a voice.
>
> The speaker was more or less human in shape but larger than a man, and so bright that I could hardly look at him. His presence smote on my eyes and on my body too (for there was heat coming from him as well as light) like the morning sun at the beginning of a tyrannous summer day.
>
> "Yes. I'm off," said the Ghost. "Thanks for all your hospitality. But it's no good, you see. I told this little chap," (here he indicated the Lizard), "that he'd have to be quiet if he came–which he insisted on doing. Of course his stuff won't do here: I realize that. But he won't stop. I shall just have to go home."
>
> "Would you like me to make him quiet?" said the flaming Spirit–an angel, as I now understood.
>
> "Of course I would," said the Ghost.
>
> "Then I will kill him," said the Angel, taking a step forward.
>
> "Oh–ah–look out! You're burning me. Keep away," said the Ghost, retreating.
>
> "Don't you want him killed?"
>
> "You didn't say anything about killing him at first. I hardly meant to bother you with anything so drastic as that."
>
> "It's the only way," said the Angel, whose burning hands were now very close to the Lizard. "Shall I kill it?"
>
> "Well, that's a further question. I'm quite open to consider it, but it's a new point, isn't it? I mean, for the moment I was only thinking about silencing it because up here–well, it's so damned embarrassing."
>
> "May I kill it?"
>
> "Honestly, I don't think there's the slightest necessity for that. I'm sure I shall be able to keep it in order now. I think the gradual process would be far better than killing it."

"The gradual process is of no use at all."

"Don't you think so? Well, I'll think over what you've said very carefully. I honestly will. In fact I'd let you kill it now, but as a matter of fact I'm not feeling frightfully well today. It would be silly to do it now. I'd need to be in good health for the operation. Some other day, perhaps."

"There is no other day. All days are present now."

"Get back! You're burning me. How can I tell you to kill it? You'd kill me if you did."

"It is not so."

"Why, you're hurting me now."

"I never said it wouldn't hurt you. I said it wouldn't kill you."

"Oh, I know. You think I'm a coward. But it isn't that. Really it isn't. I say! Let me run back by tonight's bus and get an opinion from my own doctor. I'll come again the first moment I can."

"This moment contains all moments."

"Why are you torturing me? You are jeering at me. How can I let you tear me to pieces? If you wanted to help me, why didn't you kill the damned thing without asking me–before I knew? It would be all over by now if you had."

"I cannot kill it against your will. It is impossible. Have I your permission?"

The Angel's hands were almost closed on the Lizard, but not quite. Then the Lizard began chattering to the Ghost so loud that even I could hear what it was saying.

"Be careful," it said. "He can do what he says. He can kill me. One fatal word from you and he will! Then you'll be without me for ever and ever. It's not natural. How could you live? You'd be only a sort of ghost, not a real man as you are now. He doesn't understand. He's only a cold, bloodless abstract thing. It may be natural for him, but it isn't for us. Yes, yes. I know there are no real pleasures now, only dreams. But aren't they better than nothing? And I'll be so good. I admit I've sometimes gone too far in the past, but I promise I won't do it again. I'll give you nothing but really nice dreams–all sweet and fresh and almost innocent. You might say, quite innocent...."

"Have I your permission?" said the Angel to the Ghost.

"I know it will kill me."

"It won't. But supposing it did?"

"You're right. It would be better to be dead than to live with this creature."

"Then I may?"

"Damn and blast you! Go on can't you? Get it over. Do what you like," bellowed the Ghost: but ended, whimpering, "God help me. God help me."

Next moment the Ghost gave a scream of agony such as I never heard on Earth. The Burning One closed his crimson grip on the reptile: twisted it, while it bit and writhed, and then flung it, broken backed, on the turf.

"Ow! That's done for me," gasped the Ghost, reeling backwards.

For a moment I could make out nothing distinctly. Then I saw, between me and the nearest bush, unmistakably solid but growing every moment solider, the upper arm and the shoulder of a man. Then, brighter still and stronger, the legs and hands. The neck and golden head materialized while I watched, and if my attention had not wavered I should have seen the actual completing of a man–an immense man, naked, not much smaller than the Angel. What distracted me was the fact that at the same moment something seemed to be happening to the Lizard. At first I thought the operation had failed. So far from dying, the creature was still struggling and even growing bigger as it struggled. And as it grew it changed. Its hinder parts grew rounder. The tail, still flickering, became a tail of hair that flickered between huge and glossy buttocks. Suddenly I started back, rubbing my eyes. What stood before me was the greatest stallion I have ever seen, silvery white but with mane and tail of gold. It was smooth and shining, rippled with swells of flesh and muscle, whinnying and stamping with its hoofs. At each stamp the land shook and the trees dwindled.

The new-made man turned and clapped the new horse's neck. It nosed his bright body. Horse and master breathed each into the other's nostrils. The man turned from it, flung himself at the feet of the Burning One, and embraced them. When he rose I thought his face shone with tears, but it may have been only the liquid love and brightness (one cannot distinguish them in that country) which flowed from him. I had not long to think about it. In joyous haste the young man leaped upon the horse's back. Turning in his seat he waved a farewell, then nudged the stallion with his heels. They were off before I well knew what was happening. There was riding if you like! I came out as quickly as I could from among the bushes to follow them with my eyes; but already they were only like a shooting star far off on the green plain, and soon among the foothills of the mountains. Then, still like a star, I saw them winding up, scaling what seemed

> impossible steeps, and quicker every moment, till near the dim brow of the landscape, so high that I must strain my neck to see them, they vanished, bright themselves, into the rose-brightness of that everlasting morning.

This fluent and elegant story hits the mark so well that additional comments may seem superfluous. Still, let us examine what the different symbols in the story have to do with neurotic suffering.

The ghost is a good image of the insubstantial neurotic ego and its inability to be a fully vital person. Instead of facing the dilemma of life in flesh and blood, the ghost evades conflicts by remaining without form and substance. The reality of the body has vanished into an ambiguous form that we might call "feeling anaesthesia." In contrast, what life there is resides in the lizard–the psychological complexes of the unconscious appear in a primitive, cold-blooded form to obstruct the dawning of consciousness and the development of the personality.

Jung[9] makes the following comment when talking about consciousness and suffering:

> Conscious realization . . . stops the painful content from being repressed. And though this may seem to cause the individual more suffering, he is at least suffering meaningfully and from something real. Repression has the apparent advantage of clearing the conscious mind of worry, and the spirit of all its troubles, but, to counter that, it causes an indirect suffering from something unreal, namely a neurosis. Neurotic suffering is an unconscious fraud and has no moral merit, as has real suffering.

The resulting nervousness and anxiety produces a drive to escape. In Lewis's story, the ghost was returning to hell. In life, we turn to addictions, work, exercise, overeating, drugs, and so on to distract us from the deeper issues–and often make our own hell in the process. But the sure signs of neurotic suffering are *uncertainty* and *doubt*, *equivocality* and *delay*. ("I think the gradual process would be far better than killing it.") Also, there is a certain amount of pleasure and/or a sense of security in the current condition ("I know there are no real pleasures now, only dreams. But aren't they better than nothing?"), and certainly a resistance toward transformation and a fear of change. Finally, the transformation comes along with true suffering ("Get back! You're burning me.")

Growth is painful in and of itself because our ego has to leave an entire world of illusions and become open to the reality of change and transformation. We need to discover that reality is not what we think it is or what we think it should be. We also must find that our ego is not the master in our psychic home–it does not control our personalities.

As these two illusions are challenged, we have to go through a time of desperation and agony–this agony is the passage from the death of the old into the rebirth of a new personality. As the angel broke the lizard's back, the ghost felt he was dying. But, in the end, he was transformed into a new man. Not only that, but the primal, cold blooded energy of the lizard is transformed into the warm blooded instinctual energy of the horse, which can bear the man through life and be guided by the man when he is in proper relationship to it.

The Importance of Understanding Suffering

Suffering is a topic that embraces so many aspects of our experience that it may be helpful to look at several examples or illustrative "hints" of what we are talking about. Our task in studying suffering is to go beyond classifying and to recognize what suffering has to say about the nature of human life. As a subject, it is particularly hard to understand because of its paradoxical nature. It is both inevitable and alien to us. We protect ourselves and our children against it spontaneously and yet we must find a ground not only for accepting it, but also to find meaning in it or to live through and beyond it. The following situations are helpful in amplifying this point of view.

Protecting our children and wishing for their future to be trouble-free is a timeless human indulgence. Centuries ago, Buddha's father felt the same way. His desire was to provide his son with a happy life, a high standard of living, and resources to take care of him. He wanted his son to have castles, gardens, music, and servants–an ideal life. In fact, the father had heard from prophets that his son would be either a world ruler or a world teacher, and he could not accept his son's destiny and the conflicts and sacrifices that it might contain. He tried to hide everything in the real world, the world outside their palace walls, that could turn his son's mind toward unpleasant or serious thoughts.

In a more recent case, I was asked to meet with a group of parents in a nearby college town. They were concerned about their children who were halfway through their freshman year. As a group, they were flunking out and had developed a serious drinking problem. A closer inspection revealed that most of these kids had attended fine secondary schools, often at great financial sacrifice by their parents, and had been good students. Past that point they had learned practically none of the skills of living that must be taught, practically experienced by trial and error, and worked hard at. Not a single one knew how to balance a checkbook, much less how to budget their money. Their ability to be self-disciplined and effective in the world was nonexistent. Their well-meaning, but naive parents had robbed them of the growth experiences they needed, and the result was painful, expensive, and involved dangerous emotional and physical risks.

Here we have a paradox in our developmental path. Personality and character development require developmental suffering, struggling and learning under guidance. When developmental suffering is thwarted or denied, it becomes neurotic suffering. All of us must leave the comfortable condition of unconscious living and begin making choices and suffering the resulting consequences and limitations.

In another case, I was working with a woman whose early life had been tragically marked by natural suffering. She was the oldest of three children and her mother had died of cancer when she was in her early teens. Her father, typical of his generation, was a strong, responsible, and *non-expressive* man. As the oldest child, she also became strong and responsible in order to help care for her brother and sister. In addition, she followed her father's model of being non-expressive even though she longed for his approval, comfort, and love. He worked hard and supported them well, but said little. By mid-life she couldn't remember him saying "I love you" to anyone. Throughout her difficult adolescence she had no one to talk with about her hurt, fear, anxiety, and the great trauma she had been through.

She carried this self-contained, non-expressive attitude into adulthood. The silent interior aspect of such a position is that we become alienated, self-critical, perfectionistic, and self-hating–attributes of a life lived without love.

While in her third marriage and finally with a small son, it all caught up with her and she was overwhelmed by depression. When she entered analysis, she felt that her mother's death must be her primary issue. But as we carefully put her story together and followed her dreams, we found that her unconscious energy seemed to be focused on her father. In addition to her personal concerns, she also felt hurt and angry about her father's impersonal treatment (although he did the "socially appropriate" things) of his three-year-old grandson. She wanted to feel that both she and her son were vitally important to her father.

After many teary sessions, she decided to confront him. Because she was still afraid of him and saw him as a tough old man, now eighty, she decided to write him a letter. Carefully and for many days, she worked on the letter. In it she told him how hurt she felt, how much she missed his attention, how she longed for his affirmation–for him to be proud of her, and for him to openly love and enjoy his grandson.

Before sending the letter, she decided to show it to her brother and sister. They were aghast at the idea. They replied that he was too old for such a confrontation, that he wouldn't understand it and that he wouldn't change. They suggested that she needed to work more on herself, to put the past behind her and learn to accept him as he was. They argued that he had worked hard and deserved to rest in his old age. In their defensive, conventional wisdom, they ignored the fact that he was becoming an alienated old meany, nasty to his wife and usually drunk by midafternoon.

Courageously she sent the letter anyway and waited breathlessly to see if there would be a response. There was. He was shocked at her feelings, and they had the longest and deepest conversation, with both of them in tears, of their entire life together. A few weeks after this event, her son's birthday came up. She waited to see if anything would happen from her father besides the usual savings bond coming in the mail. The bond arrived right on time; she was disappointed, but determined not to call him. Later in the afternoon she had a party for her son and his little friends. To her surprise, her father turned up as well, sober and with an armful of toys. He told her that he had planned to buy a nice educational toy, but the fact was that he hadn't been in a toy store in years. Once he got to the store, he became enthralled with the toys and spent the morning playing with them to the amusement of the clerks and some of the other customers, several of whom actually joined him. Finally he bought the ones he liked the best for his grandson. During the party, his daughter watched them play together, grandfather and four-year-old grandson, and quietly tears of joy replaced her tears of depression.

We can see that her analysis, courage, and self-understanding brought her out of or through neurotic suffering and into true suffering–suffering that had lain festering in her hidden memories and that she had tried so hard to vanquish. This movement freed her to find the deeper vitality possible in her life and a truer sense of fulfillment. It also freed both she and her father from the walls they had constructed around themselves–walls to hold out pain and, which paradoxically also held out joy and the realizations of the always new emotional potentials in life.

Such an event may seem small. Nobody's life problems were solved. But it opened a father and a daughter to reconciliation, and it opened three generations to a moment of joy, love, vitality, and a future potential beyond what any of them could have imagined a few days before. Suffering and courage take us out of the busy world of achievement and social conventions and return us to the heart of life, the home of joy.

It becomes apparent in these discussions that the cycle of life, death, and renewal and the attendant suffering is a metaphor for the psychological processes of healing and development which are based on what is often a physical reality. In the greater sense, it represents the cycle of nature as it evolves. Psychologically it is a metaphor for two kinds of transformation. It represents the process we go through developmentally as we grow from one level of consciousness to another, which is often commensurate to our stage in life. It also represents the process of psychological healing as we saw in the previous case. Natural suffering in strong or extreme cases, however, have both literal and metaphorical psychological components.

A catastrophic illness, for example, changes our bodies so radically that our personalities must completely rebuild in terms of what is now available to us and to what is required from us physically. In such a state, a *cure* is never a return to what we were before. If we think it is, or can be, we are in a state of denial. Unfortunately, our medical system and physicians rarely, if ever, define their activities to include personal change and transformation. Arthur Frank[10] speaks of our society's "prosthetic demand" that seriously ill people return to their previous lives and selves as quickly and with as little complaining as possible. This demand, supported by our medical community, acts to help us preserve our current state of denial about suffering, transformation, and the nature of life. We also are robbed of the healing power of ritual and expressive grieving once offered through mourning, groaning,[11] and the tradition of sackcloth and ashes. Losing these processes not only robs us of their healing effects, but we also lose our capacity to have such events evoke revised or unknown possibilities in our lives and true compassion for each other. Of course, when these aspects of life are denied, they return in unconscious, negative ways that we will explore later in more detail.

Catastrophic events may cause some people to batten down their psychological hatches, closing and rigidifying their conventional attitudes. Their crisis may not be interpreted as an imperative to change, but to consolidate. Older people may be particularly prone to continue adamantly on the path they have chosen, protecting themselves against the intrusion of life's mysteries and attempting to maintain their old selves until the end. For many of them this process seems to work, and we have no quarrel where it does.

Others of us find that we are faced with a truth so profound that it can only lead to a radical change in our whole way of life—for our conception of who we are and our entire idea of what life is about is turned upside down. In some cases, we may discover "who we have always been." In others, we may discover "who we may become." Sometimes these discoveries and our changes may be rapid; sometimes they may happen slowly. From the standpoint of Jungian psychology, the cutting edge questions around these issues is how much conscious participation we can marshal to put into these processes, for the responses to these situations are paradoxical and have as much or even more potential to be negative than positive.

Reynolds Price in his recent book, *A Whole New Life*, relates his devastating experience with cancer, his awful struggle with suffering, and the new self that emerged from this process. His book is one that we highly recommend, especially for people who have not had such an experience. It clearly illustrates the *primacy of experience*–what we are living through in such a case and how this experience alters the meaning structures in our lives. The primacy of the sufferer's experience is not recognized in our culture and, as Arthur Frank noted, we all pressure them to give more importance to a positive social image than to the truth they are experiencing. This shallow attitude can force suffering people into resignation, despair, and bitterness.

Reynolds Price points out that we are in these circumstances alone and must dig our own way out, that we will never get our greatest wish which is to return to who we were and that we must face the question of ". . . who we propose to be from here to the grave, which may be hours or decades down the road." His arrival at this position was a turning point in his suffering in our perspective. At this point he turned from natural suffering, which he could have abandoned himself to, and moved into the path of transcendent suffering and transformation.

From the standpoint of Jungian psychology, we could say that when Reynolds Price realized his aloneness he turned inward and rebuilt his life from his own inner foundation. This foundation is within all of us in the archetypal patterns of the collective unconscious and the Self. Within us is the inner structure needed to support us during these times and lead us to a stronger potential for healing and renewed vitality in spite of events. In the mythic sense, the hero and the sufferer are often metaphors for the same experience, and Joseph Campbell found that his mythological studies assure us that when all else is failing, we are not alone, for within us is the path that all (including sufferers) humanity has followed throughout the ages to the center of our existence and transformation.

The pattern for our struggle to understand suffering is laid out for us in the Book of Job. In page after page, Job and his advisors dialog in an effort to understand his plight. The failure to struggle to understand suffering is a failure in our effort to understand life. Such a failure limits our capacity for transformation and renewal, cuts us off from the possibility of living with vitality and joy and finally prevents us from finding a sense of completion and peace in death.

A Dynamic Perspective

This attempt at classification is our effort to get a perspective on suffering. It is not meant to be rigid, and, in fact, these classifications often interpenetrate and overlap, as do neurotic and essentially human experiences. Natural suffering reflects natural experience. Developmental suffering comes from within but is still natural. Even neurotic suffering–blockages to our development–may also be "natural" in traumatic and damaging situations. Indeed, many people have kept their creative life force alive in impossible situations through neurotic suffering.

Transforming neurotic into developmental or natural suffering is the beginning of our evolution into transcendent suffering. If we try to be too concrete in interpreting our behavior, we lessen our chance of deeper understanding, healing, and individuation. A shallow psychology (real problems rarely vanish in response to a self-help program) often thwarts and misdirects us–helping the ghost avoid his transformation. Instead, we must follow the often hard path of individuation. The step from illusion to a deeper reality is not just one step, but a series of steps, an archetypal process. Each step leads to another, and we are always pointed toward the next step in our inner development.

2

The Search For Ourselves: Suffering, Healing, and Growth Portrayed in a Fairy Tale

C.S. Lewis's story of the Ghost and the Lizard probably seemed familiar in some ways, even if you had never read it before. In the same way, myths and fairy tales also can give the impression that we know the story even if they are from a culture different from our own. This familiarity arises with fairy tales, because they reproduce typical forms of behavior and psychological patterns that appear spontaneously all over the world. These patterns are called "archetypal" in the language of Jungian psychology. They represent our inheritance: the fundamental structure that lies in the innate psychology of all humanity and guides human life and development.[1]

Myths and fairy tales help us by providing a context for our lives that is grounded in the deep, life-giving patterns of our nature. In addition, they lead us to become more attuned to and experienced in the imaginative side of our personalities, which makes the irrational aspects of life less threatening. In other words, they bring the emotional, the obscene, the grotesque, and the cruel aspects of life into relationship with our personal experience, and that relationship can be the context for a richer and broader experience of living as well as a more comforting one. Because they illustrate the elemental patterns of our nature, reading them returns us to a sense of balance between our tendency to rationally literalize life's events and the subjective nature of our inner experience. In that respect, we find that the story patterns can guide our inner development and structure over inner healing in addition to being the foundation for our attitudes and behaviors. In fact, reading them can simply help us keep our conscious and unconscious minds in balance in a manner that helps renew our vitality.

With this end in view, we would like to examine the fairy tale "Cinderella" and compare two different versions of it, one by the Brothers Grimm (1785–1863 and 1786–1859) and the other one by Charles Perrault (1628–1703). The Grimm version is supposed to be a faithful transcription of the original stories gathered from ordinary people of the time, though in fact, the Grimms occasionally combined several versions and may have edited sexuality from their tales, as did other authors. Perrault's work was intended for a more refined, aristocratic audience. He eliminated or altered details he thought vulgar or brutal in order to make the stories more palatable.

Let us compare some significant parts of these two versions.

GRIMMS[2]

The wife of a rich man fell sick, and as she felt that her end was drawing near, she called her only daughter to her bedside and said: "Dear child, be good and pious, and then the good God will always protect you, and I will look down on you from heaven and be near you." Thereupon she closed her eyes and departed. Every day the maiden went out to her mother's grave and wept; she remained pious and good. When winter came, the snow spread a white sheet over the grave, and by the time the spring sun had drawn it off again, the man had taken another wife.

The woman brought with her two daughters, who were beautiful and fair of face, but vile and

PERRAULT[3]

Once upon a time there was a gentleman who married, for his second wife, the proudest and most haughty woman that ever was seen. She had two daughters of her own, who were, indeed, exactly like her in all things. The gentleman also had a young daughter, of rare goodness and sweetness of temper, which she took from her mother, who was the best creature in the world.

The wedding was scarcely over, when the stepmother's bad temper began to show itself. She could not bear the goodness of this young girl, because it made her own daughters appear the more odious. The stepmother gave the young girl the meanest work in the black of heart. Now began a bad time for the poor stepchild. "Is the stupid goose to sit in the parlor with us?" they said. "He who wants to eat bread must earn it; out with the kitchen-wench." They took her pretty clothes away from her, put an old gray bedgown on her, and gave her wooden shoes. "Just look at the proud princess, how decked out she is!" they laughed. They sent her to the kitchen, where she worked from morning till night; she got up before daybreak, carried water, lit fires, cooked, and washed. In addition, the sisters did her every imaginable injury—they mocked her and emptied her pies and lentils into the ashes, so that she was forced to sit and pick them out again. In the evening when she had worked till she was weary, she had no bed to go to but had to sleep by the hearth in the cinders. And so because she always looked dusty and dirty, they called her Cinderella.

house to do; she had to scour the dishes and table, scrub the floors, and clean out the bedroom. The poor girl had to sleep in the garret, upon a wretched straw bed, while her sisters lay in fine rooms with inlaid floors, upon beds of the very newest fashion, and where they had looking-glasses so large that they might see themselves at their full length. The poor girl bore all patiently, and dared not complain to her father, who would have scolded her if she had done so, for his wife governed him entirely.

When she had done her work, she used to go to the chimney corner, and sit down among the cinders, hence she was called Cinderwench. The younger sister of the two, who was not so rude and uncivil as the elder, called her Cinderella. However, Cinderella, in spite of her mean apparel, was a hundred times more handsome than her sisters, though they were always richly dressed.

You may notice that the Grimm's tale opens with the illness and death of the mother. Perrault handles this scene of natural suffering in a different manner. In the Grimm version, this sad and dramatic moment offers the opportunity to praise the mother, emphasizing her loving nature and courage. This praise of the dying or dead is a typical response in the face of a fate that can neither be avoided nor overcome: It both combines and avoids the reverence for and terror of death.

The mother herself, sick and approaching death, exhibits a notable stoicism. This, too, is a typical response that often contains a certain amount of repressed anger and depression. This anger and depression shows up in the way the mother elevates herself ("I will look down on you") and transmits to her daughter a most difficult task ("be good and pious"). This task is meant to fulfill the mother's expectations and ideals–submissiveness, proper behavior, and obedience–rather than the natural tendencies of her daughter. The mother seems to embody only good qualities, but at the same time she leaves a heavy burden on her daughter.

The heritage of such a mother can have the same effect on the anima of a young man. The "anima" is Jung's term for the part of a man (which Jung took to be feminine) that connects him to his own inner self.[4] If a man has a mature anima, he can be more compassionate and gentle and also can accept his fate in a positive way. If his inner relationship to his anima is poor, he will tend to be moody, self-righteous, and ready to blame the world for his problems. This aspect of a man's psychology is formed by timeless notions of the feminine, images of women in his particular culture, and his actual emotional experiences with women, especially his mother. The experience of a mother such as Cinderella's can dominate a man's personality.

One such man, whom I worked with in analysis, had a mother who died of cancer during his adolescence. As her illness progressed over several years, she became increasingly spiritual and, to all around her, she died an inspiration and a "saint." However, as her son entered adulthood, he found himself unable to relate to more earthy women on the one hand and unable to marry for love out of his fear of loss on the other. For years his "real" relationships were lived in his fantasies while his human relationships with women were awful and destructive. He lived in reality as a "ghost."

Fritz Zorn also chronicled the potential destructiveness of this sort of spiritual burden in his book *Mars*, written during his analysis and while he was dying of throat cancer. Zorn modernizes the results of this heritage by summarizing what his parents had taught him.

> I was taught all the common Christian virtues like abstinence, renunciation, docility, patience, and, most important of all, a clear denial of almost all aspects of life. In other words, I was taught not to enjoy life but to bear it without complaint, not to be sinful but to be frustrated.[5]

Perrault's version of the Cinderella tale omits the sad and difficult confrontation with death, and opens instead with a more joyous event, the wedding of the father. Indeed, we are left to guess that there had been a death before from the reference to the "second" wife. The plot focuses on the new wife's bad temper and her two ill-tempered daughters, who present a clear contrast to the sweet nature of Cinderella. Perrault also emphasizes external characteristics such as poverty, handsomeness, and rich attire that the Grimms do not mention, while other more substantial values are neglected and thrown back into the unconscious. We can see in Perrault's "cleaning-up" of the tale a narrowing of consciousness, which begins to erode the value of the story's ability to provide an imaginal context for our lives. As Perrault moves toward the literal and the pleasing, he reduces the tale from being life-enriching to being simply entertaining and even misleading.

Ignoring painful experiences to concentrate on outward appearances doesn't make the pain go away. It keeps operating, but without the cooperation of the conscious mind, and the result is a split between the conscious and the unconscious minds. Zorn describes this split well:

> I was depressed and caught in a deepening conflict between my inner and outer life. I seemed to have no problems at all, but I was obviously finding it more and more difficult to make the image of an unproblematic life jibe with the real sense I had of myself and the world.[6]

One of the most complicated questions we face is how to know when we are really suffering. If we don't appear to be suffering, can we be suffering? If we have a stable family, a good career, a fine standing in the community, how can we be unhappy? This is often the first question people who show up in analysis must face. They are yearning, restless, and often depressed–and their spouses, friends, and often they themselves can't understand why. For whatever reason, they are losing the struggle to convince themselves they are *happy*.

So it seems the elementary psychological process of acknowledging that we're suffering is not so simple as it seems. It is a complicated, paradoxical struggle, where the ego must face the things we have denied and repressed while seeking the support of the collective unconscious (the deeper foundation of our personalities) to sustain the struggle. It is part of the human tragedy, or the Divine Comedy, whether we like it or not.

The development of the story approaches a climax after Cinderella has been to the ball and the prince is seeking the wearer of the glass slipper. In the Grimms' version, the mother is so ambitious for her daughters that she gives them a knife and even suggests that they cut their feet to fit the slipper.

GRIMMS

Then the mother gave her a knife and said: "Cut the toe off; when you are Queen, you will have no more need to go on foot." The maiden cut the toe off, forced the foot into the shoe, swallowed the pain, and went to the King's son . . . "Cut a bit off your heel; when you are Queen you will have no more . . .

PERRAULT

They began to try it on the princesses, then on the duchesses, and then all the ladies of the Court; but in vain. It was brought to the two sisters, who did all they possibly could to thrust a foot into the slippers, but they could not succeed.

Once again, the Grimm version includes the cruelty and gore of self-mutilation that Perrault omits in the name of being more civilized. Again, we might prefer Perrault's cultivated view of life, but if we want to find psychological meaning in our lives, we have to face the *cruel* process of developmental suffering and the mutilations we are vulnerable to in our development–often "for our own good."

In early life, our ego is identified with the Self. Then later, this unconscious wholeness must be broken up in order for us to develop our sense of identity in the world. As consciousness develops, we normally cut off vital parts of ourselves in order to fit parental and cultural norms and demands like the wicked sisters trimming their feet to fit the shoe. And we also may find some of our better parts sent to the cinders, denied a chance for life like Cinderella.

Later, to fulfil our development, we must make this sacrifice in reverse, that is, we must sacrifice some of our ego consciousness or hard-won identity in order to grant more reality to our inferior functions and denied aspects and the unconscious. *Inferior* in this sense doesn't mean less important, but simply less developed. And while sacrificing parts of our ego to get in touch with what we've lost is painful, there's no getting around it. We suffer to grow in whatever direction. We must let things go to grow up and then we must sacrifice some of our hard-won grown-up identity to once again become more whole. Over and over again during these complicated processes we will mutilate ourselves due to our egocentricity or the world we must adapt to.

Many people, understandably, try to rewrite their scripts and, like Perrault, they deny any cruelty and any reality of evil–and the consequences of this repression of reality and suffering are devastating for they end up violating their nature and then denying what they are doing.

Again, Zorn writes:

> At about this time, a tumor began to form on my neck. It didn't bother me because it didn't hurt and because I didn't suspect it was anything serious. I never thought that it might be cancer, and when I finally had it examined after I realized that it would not disappear but was getting larger all the time, I never imagined that the doctors would come up with any very grave diagnosis. I still had not the faintest idea of my true condition. On the one hand, I was medically ignorant; and on the other, I was clinging to my old habit of not wanting to see how truly serious my situation might be. Although I still did not know that I had a cancer, I hit intuitively on the correct diagnosis in regarding the tumor as an accumulation of "swallowed tears." What this phrase suggested to me was that all the tears that I had not wept and had not wanted to weep in my lifetime had gathered in my neck and formed this tumor because they had not been able to fulfill their true function, which was to be wept. In strictly medical terms, of course, this poetic-sounding diagnosis is beside the point. But, seen in terms of the whole person, it expresses the truth. All the suffering I had swallowed and dammed up could no longer be compressed inside me. The pressure became too great, and the resulting explosion destroyed the body containing all that compressed pain.
>
> One thing that speaks for this explanation of cancer is that there aren't any other explanations. The doctors know a great deal about cancer, but they don't know what it really is. I think that cancer is a psychic illness. If a person swallows down all his

suffering, he will eventually be eaten up in turn by the suffering buried inside of him.[7]

Zorn discovered for himself what Jung had already seen, that "Life demands for its completion and fulfillment a balance between joy and sorrow."

In the conclusion of the fairy tale we see even more clearly how the two approaches to suffering differ:

GRIMMS

When the wedding with the King's son was to be celebrated, the two false sisters came and wanted to get into favor with Cinderella and share her good fortune. When the betrothed couple went to church, the elder was at the right side and the younger at the left, and the pigeons pecked out one eye from each of them. Afterwards as they came back, the elder was at the left, and the younger at the right, and then the pigeon pecked out the other eye from each. And thus, for their wickedness and falsehood, they were punished with blindness all their days.

PERRAULT

And now her two sisters found her to be that beautiful lady they had seen at the ball. They threw themselves at her feet to beg pardon for all their ill treatment of her. Cinderella took them up, and, as she embraced them, said that she forgave them with all her heart, and begged them to love her always.

She was conducted to the young prince, dressed as she was. He thought her more charming than ever, and, a few days after, married her. Cinderella, who was as good as she was beautiful, gave her two sisters a home in the palace, and that very day married them to two great lords of the Court.

It's tempting to say that the Grimms' version suggests transformation because the negative influence of the sisters is rendered powerless, while Perrault's version seems unaware that the sisters need to be reckoned with. But this interpretation may be too simple and the endings of the stories deserve a second look.

In the Grimms' version, the emphasis is on punishment, and the punishment ties back to when the sisters cut off portions of their feet in order to obtain a position of power ("when you are a Queen you will have no more need to go on foot"). Now the greed represented by that act has indeed lost its negative influence–the sisters will no longer be able to subdue Cinderella in the old manner. But they are still and present, blinded, not killed. We might imagine that through the suffering of blindness, they may obtain the wisdom and insight that will enable them to be of future use in Cinderella's life. Their "punishment" may be a transformation in disguise. Psychologically, Cinderella joining the prince represents the emergence of a true self in the personality, while the punishment of the sisters symbolizes the depotentiation of other unhealthy psychological complexes whose energy may yet be of value as they are transformed.

If we look for a moment at the more practical aspects of personal experience, we can see how these tales can fit into our life. If we grow up in an abusive household, then to be quiet and unseen like Cinderella can be a good method of emotional survival and is functional in this dysfunctional situation. Once we are out of this family, however, the habits and conventional attitudes that were once very helpful may become a severe hinderance and we must, as Cinderella did, undergo a series of transformations and struggles to bring our full personalities to life.

Reynolds Price makes some other telling comments on transformation that resulted from his experience, but which also fit personal transformation in most instances. He notes that we must get away from Perrault's flavor of sentimentality and adopt a clear-eyed attitude toward ourselves that is as "...realistic as a sawed-off shotgun."[8]

He continues by reminding us that our mates, friends, families, and co-workers–"anyone who knew or loved you in your old life–will be hard at work to revive your old self..." It is often a shock to us that those closest to us will, like Cinderella's family, resist our transformation the most. They can find endless, practical, ethical, and even religious reasons to stall our change. Grimms' version of the tale puts these people and their efforts into true perspective and advises us that if we go on, our nature will support us.

Perrault's more purely paradisal ending shows that the situation has not only not changed much from the beginning but probably has grown worse. There is an exaggeration of courtesy, "begging pardon" and "begging love," that suggests both parties simply have adapted to a more convenient set of collective values. Cinderella seems less conscious of her own feelings at the end than she was in the beginning; and the complexes of power, envy, and egocentricity represented by the sisters are still active, reinforced, and alive beneath a socially appropriate facade. This condition reminds us of Jung's position that without the intervention of consciousness, our end is as dark as our beginning. If we view this story as a metaphor for psychological development, we find that we are still caught in a net of convention that prohibits true experience, true growth, and living as an individual and demands that we continue to live in a state of denial and unconscious illusions.

3

The Fabric of Our Lives: Suffering in Mythology

Myths like fairy tales offer us a rich and fascinating tapestry illustrating the patterns of life as they are expressed through the human imagination. They are filled with a variety of images both luminous and dark: dragons, heroes, gods, goddesses, magicians, wise old men, wise old women, and many others. In a fundamental way, the primordial images in myths give us a perspective on who we are, what we would like to be, and where we belong psychologically. If we can understand and assimilate these images in our personal psychology, they can inform our living experience, grounding our personal stories in the larger story of humankind. For, after all, our psyche is not just personal. It also has characteristics common to all humans, and arises in the context of an impersonal and objective nature.

In this way, myths do more than entertain; they can help us with our process of transformation. Through the myth, the dynamic archetypal images of the collective unconscious become visible to our conscious mind, and can provide a thread that we may follow through the labyrinth of our own experience. In this manner, they can help keep us from drowning in or being possessed by life experiences or the conventional attitudes that we must differentiate from.

We have selected two different myths to study, from two ancient cultures, rich in aesthetics and significant in the founding of the civilization we know. The first is the Sumerian myth of Inanna as presented by Diane Wolkstein and Samuel Noah Kramer, and the second the Greek myth of Prometheus, as offered by Aeschylus. These two myths offer us a broader and more intense perspective on our development than we normally have. In the first one, the descent Inanna, we see an imaginal version of the journey toward identity and the development of the feminine in women, or perhaps the anima in men. In a similar manner, Prometheus depicts a process in the development of the basic masculine identity in men, or in another vein the animus in women. The animus is Jung's term for the hypothetical masculine component in a woman's personality. The psychological function of the animus is to connect a woman to her deeper self. If she has a mature connection to this part of herself, she will have a more comfortable sense of self-authority and a feeling of her own voice when interacting and dealing with the world. A positive relationship with the animus facilitates achievement and a feeling of confidence. A negative relationship with it leads to an effort to dominate situations based on a deep feeling of anxiety and inadequacy. This aspect of a woman's psychology is formed by the timeless notions of the masculine, cultural images, and her actual emotional experiences of men, especially her father.

Both myths also may be imagined to represent metaphors of collective development as well. Most importantly, they suggest different ways of experiencing suffering that are significant for all of us. One way takes place in the depths of the underworld, and the other in the openness of sunlight. They differ from each other as winter differs from summer, but both have a momentous part in the same deep, human cycle of suffering.

Heart and Body: Inanna as an Image of Suffering in the Transformation of the Feminine Soul

Descent into the depths is a theme that appears in different forms practically all over the world: Ulysses descends to consult Tiresias, Dante journeys with Virgil, Faust goes down with

Mephistopheles. This common motif expresses the psychological mechanism of introversion, when the conscious mind turns inward toward deeper layers of the unconscious. Usually, the heroes of the myths return to the world of the living with great treasures, reminding us that we can find the precious inner treasure by taking a difficult journey to a dangerous place. As Joseph Campbell notes:

> Furthermore, we have not even to risk the adventure alone, for the heroes of all time have gone before us. The labyrinth is thoroughly known. We have only to follow the thread of the hero path, and where we had thought to find an abomination, we shall find a god. And where we had thought to slay another, we shall slay ourselves. Where we had thought to travel outward, we will come to the center of our own existence. And where we had thought to be alone, we will be with all the world.[1]

Inanna's descent into the underworld began when she "opened her ear to the Great Below."[2] It is not completely clear why she decided to undertake this journey, but since the words "ear" and "wisdom" are the same in Sumerian, we can guess that she is responding to a sort of "call" for further self-development. Depression was both the call and the descent for the woman we discussed in Chapter Two whose mother had died early in her life. You may remember that while this woman was outwardly successful, she had become so self-contained that she was split off from herself and others. Psychologically, we could surmise that Inanna opened herself to her own depths or unconscious. This opening also means that she became more aware of her shadow, her sister Ereshkigal.

As our identities develop, adapting to the situation around us, we have to repress the parts of our personalities that don't fit our circumstances. These repressed characteristics–which often include some of the darker aspects of human nature–remain in our personal unconscious to form what Jungians call the *shadow.* These attributes often slip out when we are anxious, emotionally exhausted, or drunk. In other words, when our guard is down.

Someone who develops in a wounding or limiting environment (so this is a problem we all face to some extent) may repress some of their best characteristics into their shadow. There may be an assertive, competent person living in the shadow of a shy individual with low self-esteem, or a tender and compassionate person in the shadow of the hard-driving business person. We need a shadow to be a person of substance, a three dimensional person. To embrace life with vitality, we must acknowledge sides of our nature that we have previously denied. If we cannot face this struggle, then we are sentenced to living a surface existence, but if we can, we find that instead of becoming fragmented we become more unified and instead of becoming drained we become energized. The result is an enhanced sense of life. Inanna is on this type of inward journey.

Inanna's journey begins slowly. She must pass through seven gates, one at a time. With each passage, she must relinquish some part of her surface power and prestige–her glory, her cities, her castles, her crown, and her jewels. She must abandon everything in her descent to the spiritual realm of the underworld except her determination to be reborn. Psychologically, she is letting go of what she thought of as her identity in order to face her own truth without illusions about herself.

The surface identity that Inanna had to relinquish was what Jungians call the *persona.* Our persona is the mask we use to represent ourselves to the world. Commonly, we use our persona to gain us social approval and like it to coincide with our idea of how we should appear in public. It's a presentable alternative to our unpresentable shadow. But until we accept our shadow, our persona is usually an illusion–who we think we are rather than who we are.

Once we become aware of our shadow we also may become more aware of our persona as something separate from our true self. By acknowledging our shadow, we become more than our persona. This lets us use our persona to express more of our true personality and particular interests in the world. But make no mistake. As the myth clearly points out, this task of coming to grips with the shadow side of ourselves is difficult and is often experienced as an emotional journey into hell. It means giving up the illusions that we have so carefully constructed over the years, especially the fantasy of who we are.

Dante[3] noted the pain of this descent in his description of the sign over the gate to the Inferno.

> Through me the way into the suffering city, through me the

> way to the eternal pain, through me the way that runs among the lost. Justice urged on my high artificer; my maker was divine authority, the highest wisdom, and the primal love. Before me nothing but eternal things were made, and I endure eternally. Abandon every hope, who enter here.

Inanna's passage through seven gates has special symbolic significance. Seven is associated with the idea of a slow, cyclical process in time–the seven planets, the seven days of the week–and when seven is completed, a new cycle begins. The myth thus informs us that we need patience for inner work, and inner transformations can only take place when we give ourselves the time required to complete the cycle of our personal growth.

Such inner journeys also require intense courage. Dante[4] on reading the sign at the gateway says:

> These words–their aspect was obscure–I read inscribed above a gateway, and I said: "Master, their meaning is difficult for me." And he to me, as one who comprehends: "Here one must leave behind all hesitation; here every cowardice must meet its death."

Inanna seems to be aware of the danger in her descent. She takes the precaution of instructing her female assistant Ninshubur to appeal to the father gods for help in case she does not come back within three days–another sign of the resurrection cycle.

Though Inanna is determined to expose herself to the "fearful unknown," she is conscious that her strength may not be enough. So she wants someone in the Upper World, some conscious aspects of herself, to be able to come to her aid.

The need for support beyond our own strength is often important when we are thinking about beginning an inner journey. A successful, professional man who had become interested in Jungian psychology came into analysis because he had the following dream. He was about to cross the threshold into a dark basement in his childhood home. As he put his foot out, a large hand or force grabbed him and whisked him back. He decided he should not proceed without the guidance and help of an analyst.

Once again, Dante illustrates the need of a guide when he loses his senses at the end of Canto III. He awakes in Canto IV and finds himself on the edge of an abyss. His guide, Virgil[5] says to him, "I shall go first and you will follow me." The unconscious and the inner journey can be dangerous if we approach it with overconfidence. Even Jung[6] himself noted that he needed the contact with ordinary life, family, and profession as a touchstone while confronting his unconscious.

As he once wrote, "Every therapist ought to have a control by some third person, so that he remains open to another point of view. Even the Pope has a confessor."[7]

Jung also gives the example of the value of a guide. A physician he worked with began having dreams that indicated a latent psychosis. Jung ended the analysis and sent the man on his way in such a manner as to leave his unconscious undisturbed. He thought that the confrontation would be shattering for the man rather than uniting and growthful. Without the thoughtful and sensitive insight of Jung, his guide, this man may have destroyed his life by naively pursuing the wrong journey.

Inanna's sister Ereshkigal, whose husband's death prompted her journey, is the queen of the Great Below. But before being relegated to the netherworld, she was a grain goddess who lived above. Ereshkigal thus represents the energy connected with the process of decay and gestation–the seed that goes into the earth in order to die and sprout again. Our ancestors honored this process through rituals where the death of one's previous identity was symbolized as a passage to a superior level of existence.[8]

Today we no longer perform transformative rituals as a culture. We don't prepare the ritual dances and ceremonies to stir up our energies for transformation.[9] Instead, those psychic energies reside in the unconscious and are expressed in fear, anxiety, rage, destructiveness, or if we try to avoid the confrontation, a depression that we try to deny and repress.

The analytic setting recreates many of the characteristics of the ancient rituals. People meet with their analyst on the same day, the same hour, and at the same place which creates a ritual space in the tempo of today's pressured living. The process of analysis, with its focus on our dreams and fantasies, and its journey into our deep past, is similar to the journeys and ordeals enacted symbolically in the ancient rites. And when we leave analysis, we are transformed, endowed with new knowledge and experience. Perhaps the yearning for such a change is the motivation, or the hope, that induced Inanna to undertake her descent.

A woman once came to see me for a period of months because of a terrifying feeling of anxiety that she could not control. She was so frightened of her unconscious that she was only able to sleep for two or three hours a night. She tried to defend against her terror by constantly staying active and busy. She seldom remembered dreams and often it was difficult to find something to talk about in the analytic hour, because she always said everything was fine, even though this was obviously not the case. For a period of time, I believed that each session might be the last.

But she kept coming. Indeed, she came so regularly that I could practically set the clock by the sound of the doorbell at her arrival. Coming to analysis gave her the sensation of being in a place far from this world, a place where time and space were not important. This ritual withdrawal from the world gave her hope for a change that she could not envision in her daily life and began the healing process, nurturing the seed at a deeper level than we could discuss.

But paradoxically the story notes that Ereshkigal opposes Inanna's visit. In fact, she is so furious that she wants Inanna treated according to the laws of the underworld. As a result, Inanna is killed and hung from a hook on the wall. Inanna now appears to be beyond help. She is at an impasse, suspended, and deadlocked–in short, in the state that Jung considered the typical beginning for the individuation process–the state that we are in when our lives seem deadlocked.

Ereshkigal represents the neglected side of Inanna, including her instinctive, compulsive, insatiable, and sexual characteristics. Ereshkigal also includes the wounded and frightened parts of Inanna, the parts Inanna had rejected from her conscious identity, striping them of respect and reverence and a place in her life. It's not surprising that, in these circumstances, these denied parts might become an adversary whose aim is to kill and destroy. But bear in mind that the ancients thought that death is the separation of body and spirit. If we take this into account, we can understand the murderous response of Ereshkigal–it is the anguished response of our nature that results from psychic splitting.

Ereshkigal is unloving and unloved, abandoned and lonely, even destructive. But, as we will see as the story unfolds, she is also pregnant. Soon she will go through the fundamental human experience of labor and birth. Ereshkigal, who appeared to be so terrible and savage, is in fact ready to bring forth a new life.

While Inanna was in the underworld, the earth was barren and nothing grew or reproduced. This barrenness while the heroine is in the underworld also appears in the myth of Persephone when she was trapped in the underworld by Hades.

> The earth would not send up a single sprout, for Demeter of the lovely crown kept the seed covered. In vain, the oxen dragged the many curved ploughs through the fields and much white barley was sown in the earth to no avail.[10]

This situation is characteristic of analytical work during a deep depression. Our instinctual life has often been suffocated by our persona and relegated into the unconscious, where it turns negative and destructive. Our life's energy and vitality is blocked, trapped in an abyss of hopelessness and loneliness that is protected by a rigid wall of defensive fear. Then, as we come to understand the symbolic aspects of life, we can rebuild the bridge between the conscious and unconscious that was destroyed or lost. Our personalities can move forward with an evolution of those forces that have been still and stagnant.

A quotation from Jung in one of his letters fits with our discussion.

> Dear N., I am sorry you are so miserable. "Depression" means literally "being forced downwards." This can happen even when you don't consciously have any feeling at all of being "on top." So I wouldn't dismiss this hypothesis out of hand . . . When the darkness grows denser, I would penetrate to its very core and ground, and would not rest until amid the pain a light appeared to me, for in *excessu affectus* Nature reverses herself. I would turn in rage against myself and with the heat of my rage I would melt my lead. I would renounce everything and engage in the lowest activities should my depression drive me to violence. I would wrestle with the dark angel until he dislocated my hip. For he is also the light and the blue sky which he withholds from me.[11]

When Inanna does not return after three days, her assistant

Ninshubur goes to the "fathers" and pleads for help. Enil and Nanna, Inanna's grandfather and father, both refuse to help her and don't appreciate or even understand the journey she's going through. But the god Enki, her mother's father, agrees to help her. Enki is the god of wisdom and waters, and at the beginning of the story has been struggling with Ereshkigal.[12] Even though Inanna had gotten him drunk and stolen the *me* (the ordering principle that applied to both gods and men) from him for her people, he did not forget that she was queen of heaven and earth and that her existence was vital to all the lands.

With great wisdom, Enki takes the dirt from under his fingernails and from it creates two small creatures the size of flies. They are the "kurgarra" and the "galatur," professional mourners capable of mirroring lonely Ereshkigal's emotions. As professionals, brought in to mourn for others, they represent collective, objective expressions of the sorrow of life rather than personal or individual sorrows. Often they express sorrow for those aspects of life that society considers poor, mediocre, and so irrelevant that they are not even perceived. We need these creatures and what they symbolize for the full experience of living. By their concern, they calm the pain of the anguished queen and she becomes willing to offer fertility and growth in return for their empathy.

Instead, they ask her to release the part of her personal anguish, despair, and anger, embodied in Inanna–a part of herself that she did not want to mention. Now that Ereshkigal had experienced the help, pleasure, and rapport with the "other" that she had been split away from, she was able to release part of her pain. In a sense, there seems to be a role reversal here, but we must remember that both Inanna and Ereshkigal represent two parts of a single personality that have been split from each other, and both still have its emotional and suffering component.

Released, Inanna is reborn with the water and food of life given to her by the two messengers of Enki. But before leaving the underworld, she must agree to provide someone to take her place. At this point in the myth, a passage has been created between the Great Above and the Great Below–a connection between the conscious and the unconscious–and Inanna will not forget Ereshkigal, the sister who is a true part of herself.

Inanna leaves the underworld, bringing with her the demons whose job it is to bring back her substitute. As soon as she reaches the surface, they decide to take her faithful assistant Ninshubur, but Inanna wants to make a more deliberate decision and refuses. She then discovers that while she was in the underworld, her two sons and her servants abandoned their routine life and put on their garments of mourning. She does not want any of them to go and take her place. However, her husband Dumuzi did not seem to miss her very much. Dumuzi, the King of Sumer, simply sat on the royal throne wearing the noble *me*-garments that his wife had given to him, ruling the kingdom without being too worried about her absence.

The encounter between the King and Queen of Sumer seems to symbolize the two different ways of ruling our lives. We can imagine Dumuzi as being rational and superficial, oriented toward achievement and practicality. He might claim that he was ruling the kingdom and doing all the work while his wife was adventuring in the chaos of the underworld. And now, if she is tormented by the demons of the underworld after searching for a deeper life, well, that's her problem, not his.

Inanna, on the other hand, has just completed a deep and intense journey and gained new knowledge that goes beyond concrete reality. She had loved Dumuzi, but while she went to the underworld to seek out the most vital aspects of her own life, he took advantage of her absence and usurped her power. He showed only enough love to be able to use her.

"Inanna fastened on Dumuzi the eye of death," as the myth says, and the demons went to seize him. He escaped from the demons and stumbled across the steppe, but he then had a dream that terrified him. He didn't understand the meaning and sought help from his wise sister, Geshtinanna, who told him his dream announced a terrible destiny–that the two of them, first one and then the other, would be taken away to the underworld.

They both became grief-stricken and tried to escape, even though they knew they couldn't avoid their destiny. Inanna wept for her husband, but Dumuzi had to go. Still, because his sister shared his fate, he only had to spend half the year in the underworld, with his sister there for the other half. The myth ends with a statement that

Dumuzi was "placed in the hands of the eternal" and with a song to the holy Ereshkigal and to her great renown.

What further meaning for our study of suffering can we glean from the myth of Inanna, Queen of Sumer? There is Inanna's determination to complete her womanhood and queenship in a compassionate way. Despite all the difficulties and trials she faces and all the tears she sheds, she is able to remain consistent and pursue the truth about herself. A deep spontaneous ardor guides her to the underworld, a journey that another type of consciousness, one more factual and rational like that of her husband, always tries to avoid. The inner journey this ardor inspires leaves her in a state of outer inertia, shown in the myth when the land above is barren. When our vitality disappears from our consciousness, we can't ignore the problem by keeping ourselves busy with different distractions. Sooner or later we find ourselves stumbling across the steppe like Dumuzi, trying to escape the demons from the underworld.

We need to find a solution. Sometimes this solution comes through a laborious, patient period of waiting. We simply wait for what the unconscious has to tell us about the situation. Sometimes we must engage in an active search for those energies lost in the hidden places of the unconscious, guided by the help of an analyst who has already experienced the night journey–as Enki, who had already struggled with Ereshkigal, was able to help Inanna.

Esther Harding comments on this situation in her discussion of psychic energy:

> If we don't realize that new forces must be mobilized to meet new situations, we superstitiously expect a new attitude to be available as though by magic. This new attitude, however, must arise from the unconscious before it can be made available for the life situation, and this requires a creative act that takes time.[13]

A medical doctor in his forties, after a successful career, decided to leave his practice and become a Jungian analyst. He went back to college to study psychiatry and then to the Jung Institute for a brief period. He felt as if he was following a destiny that belonged to him. Meanwhile, his marriage ended in divorce, which increased both his suffering and his obligations. As is often the case, his destiny revealed itself as harder to follow than he thought. Presently, he ran short of money and decided the pain was simply too much, and the goal too far into the future.

He decided to go to work in a psychiatric clinic where he could make enough money to balance his financial situation. In return, he had to accept a compromise that, after so much anguish, seemed easy–to work as a typical institutional psychiatrist, using medications to treat symptoms and denying the symbolic life he had started to discover. But after only a few months of working in that clinic, he began having a recurring nightmare. This dream became so all-consuming that, when one of his patients mentioned a dream to him, the psychiatrist immediately obsessed so much on his own dream that he could not follow what his patient was saying. In his own dream, he had to go into a niche in a wall that was too narrow for him, so narrow that he could not move and he could only see a feeble light. In the dream he was saying, "I have to do it one more time, just one more time . . ."

With the help of his own analyst, he became aware that it wasn't money he needed in order to go on with his life. He needed more genuine energy to help him endure the suffering and get through his own wasteland. He couldn't maintain the same standard of living that he had before and had to face some changes. He spoke openly with his children, and from that discussion, he started having a more sincere relationship not only with them but also with himself. He found the ardor, determination, and compassion of Inanna.

Mind and Consciousness: Prometheus as an Image of Suffering in the Transformation of the Masculine Spirit

In the early mythology of Greece, the story of Prometheus symbolized the process, suffering, and sacrifice that both depicted mankind's predicament and the transformation of this position into something more exquisite, refined, and godlike–in psychological terms more conscious. In these stories, Prometheus was a titan whose name meant "forethought" or "foresight." In contrast, his brother's name, Epimetheus, meant "afterthought" or "hindsight." As his name indicated, Prometheus could foretell the future. In addition, some scholars have suggested that his name may have been a

Grecianized form of the Sanskrit word "Promantha" meaning "fire-stick."

Prometheus appears in a much longer mythological history. Hesiod,[14] writing in the seventh century B.C., described five races of man corresponding to the five ages of the world. The first was a golden age, consisting of eternal springtime. During this age, the soil produced so abundantly that toil was unnecessary. Men were good and felt content. They knew neither poverty nor strife. Death came to them after a very long life and seemed like falling into a peaceful sleep.

In the next age, the silver age, Zeus created the seasons with the resultant hunger and cold. Houses had to be built and clothes made. Men showed courage in their adversity, but frequently became overbearing and forgot to pay homage to the gods. As a result, Zeus swept them off the face of the earth and resolved to create a new race. Then Zeus, with the help of Prometheus, took some clay from the banks of the river Arcadia and shaped it into the likeness of the gods. Then he breathed the breath of life into the figures he had created, thus forming the new race of mankind.

In contrast to the gods and goddesses, this new race was mortal and subject to suffering and death. The gods instructed Prometheus and Epimetheus to give the new races the attributes they needed. Lacking wisdom and foresight, Epimetheus gave power to the animals, leaving man defenseless and naked. Prometheus felt sorry for man and wanted to give him fire. He reasoned that, with fire, man would not need to fear the dark and cold and could make tools and weapons. Zeus, however, feared that if man was given fire, he would think of himself as equal to the gods, so he refused to grant the titan's request.

Aeschylus[15] presents an even more complex version of how man ended up without fire. One day there was a dispute among men as to which part of the sacrificial victim was to be given to the gods. Prometheus devised a plan for settling the dispute. After skinning the animal, he put the poor skin on the good meat. Then he took the bones and covered them with the good skin and appetizing fat and let Zeus choose which of the sacrifices he preferred. The king of the gods rejected the best part that had been skillfully concealed, and this best portion was givento men.

Zeus was enraged when he discovered that he had been outwitted, so he took fire away from man and reduced him to eating raw meat. Feeling sorry for man, Prometheus then stole fire from Olympus and brought it to earth in a fire-stick. Zeus punished him for this defiance by chaining him to a pillar at the top of a mountain in the Caucasus. There an eagle pecked out his immortal liver every day, and every night it renewed itself, producing a cycle of endless agony.

But Zeus's anger was still not spent, and he devised another calamity for man. Zeus instructed Hephaistos to make the first woman out of the mud of the earth. Athena gave her knowledge of the arts and adorned her with beauty, Aphrodite covered her head with loving charm and consuming desire, and the Graces contributed to her elegance. Hermes armed her with cunning and flattery and placed dishonesty in her heart. Thus she combined allure and deceit, an evil woman whom all men would desire. This woman was Pandora, whose name meant the "bearer of every gift."

Despite the warnings of Prometheus not to accept gifts from Zeus, Epimetheus was so smitten that he welcomed Pandora to the world of mortals. Pandora brought a jar with her that Zeus had warned her never to open. When she could resist her curiosity no longer, she lifted the lid for a quick look at its secrets. In that fateful moment, all the miseries of man flew out into the world: greed, vanity, slander, envy, and the other deadly vices. Horrified, Pandora slammed the lid of the box and retained for man only *elpis*, hope. Man is left with hope and also the eternal quandary of whether hope is our most basic virtue, or one of the vices that failed to escape.

In the myth as handed down by Aeschylus in *Prometheus Bound*, our hero narrates his love for mankind and tells of his gifts to them:

> (Prometheus) From thoughts of coming death I saved mankind.
> (Leader) What medicine for that sickness couldst thou find?
> (Prometheus) Blind hopes I planted in their hearts to dwell.
> (Leader) A blessed thing for lives so miserable!
> (Prometheus) And further... I gave Fire to them that die.
> (Leader) And hath man Fire, that bright all-piercing eye?
> (Prometheus) Whence he shall learn all arts, all greatnesses.[16]

So what does this myth tell us about the psychology of suffering? In the myth, fire is the divine spark that enables us to rise above the animals and the mud, the nature from which we originated. The divine spark, the conscious rational mind including reflection and intuition, is the treasure we have received from Prometheus. The eagle, a royal bird of prey, announces the prestige of the gift of consciousness. But this golden bird also inflicts a slow and rending pain every single day to our body, which is forever split between mind and nature.

Yet the liver–the source of blood for the body, and in ancient times the seat of destiny–is restored each night to renew the vitality of mankind. This symbolic process closely parallels the healing we experience during the "night repair" of dreams.

Prometheus' torment represents developmental suffering, one of the fundamental facts of human life that cannot be changed. This suffering is the price of consciousness, the light and warmth of human life; while we are in the process of individuation, our ego must remain motionless, bearing the tension and enduring the pain. Only then can there be hope that one day, from the central core of the Self, salvation will come as the mature Heracles came in the myth.

Prometheus, in a generous deed of love, gave us the energy to live our lives with enthusiasm and the capacity to build a better future by the means of sacrifice and pain. With his vital gift, stolen from the sun, Prometheus set us on the pathway of dignity and value. We are meant to live with the same passion he showed in his heroic act, to experience a passionate suffering that goes deep into the heat of strong emotions, burning away all the superficialities that keep us from being whole. Such passion purifies the ground of our being and transforms us. By an audacious act of love, Prometheus intervened and made a difference in the destiny of man. This act precedes or perhaps foretells another act of love, a love that "bears all things" and "endures all things" and that changed the destiny of the world as well.

Fire, offering warmth and light and often searing, transforming heat, is often used to express the various shades of love. Theseshades range from the most delicate and impalpable to the strongest and most tenacious. "Love is as strong as death, its jealousy unyielding as the grave. It burns like blazing fire, like a mighty flame" (Song of Songs 8:6). In the symbolism of fire, consciousness and love are summarized and united in a dangerous and apparently absurd paradox that is as strong and eternal as death. In *Aion*, Jung expresses clearly the various aspects and meanings associated with fire:

> Fire means passion, affects, desires, and the emotional driving-forces of human nature in general, that is, everything which is understood by the term "libido." When the alchemists attribute a quaternary [four-fold] nature to the fire, this amounts to saying that the self is the source of energy.[17]

In the Promethian myth, fire as consciousness also brings on the wrath of Zeus. Prometheus struggles with defiant determination against his oppressor, never abandoning his love for mankind. The inexorable Zeus, powerful and harsh, must grow soft if he wants to maintain his scepter because Prometheus, through foresight, knows the secret which can dethrone him–that the sea-goddess, Thetis, is destined to bear a son greater than his father. As you may suppose, Zeus intended to make Thetis his bride.

This foresight gives Prometheus his power, and the power of such knowledge is greater than a kingdom. If Zeus can come to terms with him, his kingdom will be transformed. Zeus will learn benevolence, wisdom, and maturity, enabling his reign to continue, and in fact, the mythology of ancient Greece shows Zeus maturing over time. A similar pattern can be seen in Jahweh in the *Old Testament.*

And Prometheus will also gain something in this exchange: He will be released by Heracles, who will shoot down the eagle with his arrow. Then the gentle centaur, Chiron, will take over his suffering and start the field of medicine, which Asclepias will then refine into a high and noble art.

Certainly suffering, in the eternal and archetypal sense, has meaning. If we have determination and courage, suffering can become the teacher of life in the higher sense. The suffering of Prometheus transforms Zeus and, in fact, the figures in the myth interact and transform each other. Likewise, when we participate in their very human condition, learning through suffering, we can not only transform ourselves but also have an effect on those around us, who participate in compassion. Zeus learned wisdom and mercy from Prometheus, and the two of them were reconciled in the end.

This is not to say that learning through suffering is easy. Often it is so hard that we are tempted to find a *scapegoat* on whom to discharge our guilt. Such is the case with Pandora who with her wiles and fatal curiosity is blamed for all human misery. Of course, blaming Pandora is a superficial solution to the problem of guilt and responsibility. This oversimplification encourages a terrible and dangerous misunderstanding that reduces "archetypes" to "stereotypes," turning eternal and profound themes into short simple formulas. Instead, we must accept the responsibility of being conscious, even though that responsibility brings developmental pain with it.

C.G. Jung points out that higher consciousness can bring with it not only pain, but also the danger of inflation and loneliness:

> This phenomenon, which results from the extension of consciousness, is in no sense specific to analytical treatment. It occurs whenever people are overpowered by knowledge or by some new realization. "Knowledge puffeth up," Paul writes to the Corinthians, for the new knowledge had turned the heads of many, as indeed constantly happens. The inflation has nothing to do with the kind of knowledge, but simply and solely with the fact that any new knowledge can so seize hold of a weak head that he no longer sees and hears anything else. He is hypnotized by it, and instantly believes he has solved the riddle of the universe. But that is equivalent to almighty self-conceit. This process is such a general reaction that, in Genesis 2:17, eating of the tree of knowledge is represented as a deadly sin. It may not be immediately apparent why greater consciousness followed by self-conceit should be such a dangerous thing. Genesis represents the act of becoming conscious as a taboo infringement, as though knowledge meant that a sacrosanct barrier had been impiously overstepped. I think that Genesis is right insofar as every step towards greater consciousness is a kind of Promethean guilt: through knowledge, the gods are as it were robbed of their fire, that is, something that was the property of the unconscious powers is torn out of its natural context and subordinated to the whims

> of the conscious mind. The man who has usurped the new knowledge suffers, however, a transformation or enlargement of consciousness, which no longer resembles that of his fellow men. He has raised himself above the human level of his age ("ye shall become like unto God"), but in so doing has alienated himself from humanity. The pain of this loneliness is the vengeance of the gods, for never again can he return to mankind. He is, as the myth says, chained to the lonely cliffs of the Caucasus, forsaken of God and man.[18]

The last image, beautifully described by Jung, presents another aspect of developmental suffering. Prometheus, as "forethought," could also represent the intuitive type who has to be chained to the rock of material existence because of his creative nature. It reminds us of many painters (Van Gogh), or musicians (J.S. Bach, W.A. Mozart), or writers (Dickens, Twain) who had to confront the financial problems of everyday life while also responding to the creative need that flowed from their hearts.

There is no other way to solve this problem except by bearing the terrible tension that the reality of human life involves. As Eric Fromm reiterated, the mind is both a blessing and a curse. But it is here we find the challenge offered by suffering: The path between conflicting impulses leads us to a destination we can neither see nor imagine, but we know from our deeper Self guides us to our own destiny.

Medicine, the noble art that, through the centaur Chiron traces back to the suffering of Prometheus, is symbolized by the Caduceus,[19] a wand with two serpents twined around it, surmounted by two small wings or a winged helmet. The serpent has a double symbolic aspect, good and evil, and the caduceus shows both in their antagonism and their equilibrium, spiraling together around the axis mundi, the symbolic center of life.

This commanding symbol, whose power seems lost today, shows us that health has a deeper meaning, a meaning of the soul that rests on the totality of our being. The arduous journeys of Inanna and Prometheus inform us that we must individually undertake the journey through life's dualities until we can discriminate the meaning and value of the smallest thing or image as unique and valuable. Then we can become aware of one of the

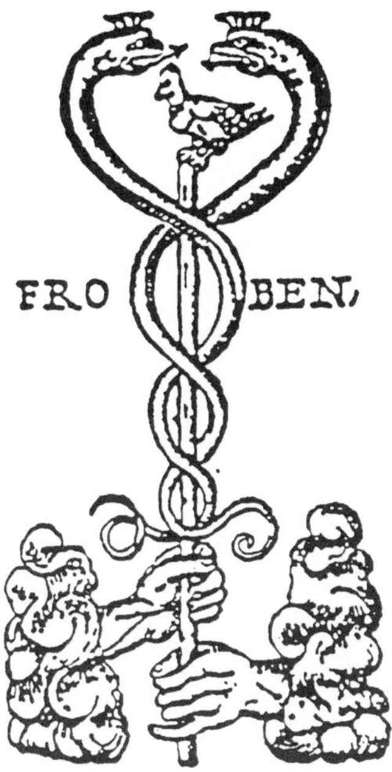

Caduceus (Swiss, 1515).

Early Sumerian version of the Caduceus.

central secrets of life, that is, through consciousness earned through suffering we are able to recognize the gifts of life reserved for those who truly live. And the health of the soul is realized through self-knowledge grounded in our instinctual selves. This is the point at which we can genuinely begin to learn about ourselves and the meaning of life.

4

Fire and Emptiness: A Brief Perspective on Suffering in Religions

In the past century or so, we have tried to replace the old religious and philosophical structures with the notion that through science and reason we can overcome nature and eliminate suffering. Instead we have found that, not only does suffering persist, but the science that was to save us has produced new forms of it: As Jung wrote:

> The thread by which our fate hangs is wearing thin. Not nature, but the 'genius of mankind' has knotted the hangman's noose with which it can execute itself at any moment.[1]

Philosophical and religious belief systems have helped people struggle with suffering since human beginnings, and these systems can still help us find the meaning in suffering even when it seems impossible or absurd that such meaning could exist. Religious structures can help us not only endure pain but transform it into a healing system or even a way of redemption. When stricken with grief, we may (as our ancestors did) question the purpose of life and look for meaning in a universe that harbors such pain. Religions, in a broad sense, have worked out answers to these questions.

In one of his letters, Jung wrote:

> I believe that misery is an intrinsic part of human life,

> without which we would never do anything. We always try to escape misery . . . If anybody achieves at least endurance of misery, he has already accomplished an almost superhuman task. This might give him some happiness or satisfaction. If you call this happiness, I wouldn't have much to say against it . . . (note) Man has to cope with the problem of suffering. The Oriental wants to get rid of suffering by casting it off. Western man tries to suppress suffering with drugs. But suffering has to be overcome, and the only way to overcome it is to endure it. We learn that only from him. And here he pointed to the Crucified.[2]

So how have the three major western religions–Judaism, Christianity, and Islam–dealt with suffering? Of course, we could easily write an entire book on each of these religions, but for this work we have simply outlined them and added a quick look at the Yoga and Buddhist contributions as well. If you wish to pursue any of these religions further in your own studies, we would suggest that you begin with Mircea Eliade's *Encyclopedia of Religion.*

Judaism

Judaism is the religion of the Jewish people from the manifestations of God at Sinai to the present day, and its influence has now spread throughout the world. Judaism professes to believe in one asexual, eternal, creator God. This God is a righteous and compassionate judge who entered into a permanent, historical relationship with the "Children of Israel," that would culminate in redemption at the end of time.

The suffering of the Jewish people also has been significant in world affairs for centuries. Judaism considers suffering to be the natural result of mankind's vulnerability–suffering arises simply from the fact of being human. Sometimes suffering may result from following the wrong path. In that case, it is both a consequence of and a punishment for sin or ignorance. From the standpoint of analytical psychology, we generally may compare this type of suffering to neurotic suffering. Sin may be contrasted to a dissociation from our true personality, a split from ourselves and the Self (often considered the image of God within). Clearly such a psychological state also results, in many cases, from following the wrong developmental path, and sin in this case represents acts of self-alienation. This type of suffering may combine with a second type of suffering, which attends spiritual progress. In this instance suffering has a purifying purpose. "And now I have put you in the fire like silver, I have tested you in the furnace of distress (Isaiah 48:10)."

The psychological analogy to this second type of suffering is more complex. In a developmental sense, spiritual progress begins with the differentiation of a personality. We must first become a person in order to become a spiritual person. Therefore, the first step in spiritual progress is developmental suffering. Then the personality must go through a process of suffering that gives up the egocentric ideas that result from individual development and serve a higher calling. In psychology, this means to give up our egocentric position in life in service of the Self. Therefore, we have a continuum of suffering as we follow the individuation process that is similar to the suffering in spiritual progress. Psychologically, in this process, developmental suffering flows into transcendent suffering. The second implication in this tradition involves natural suffering. In the context of spiritual refinement, natural suffering is an imperative to seek the meaning in suffering–it is an imperative to seek transcendent suffering in the events of affliction.

A misconception about truth also can cause suffering by leading to self-destructive rather than self-fulfilling actions. The stories of Jacob and Joseph show that self-knowledge and an understanding of the world come only through struggle, and we become sensitive to life in a new way for having suffered. As the story of Jacob begins in the Old Testament, we find the egocentric ingredients of greed, power, and deception being continually acted out. They culminate as he deceives his aging father and steals his brother's blessing, the promise of land and plenty. His egocentricity results in fraternal strife, conflict with neighboring tribes, and having to move from place to place.

If we consider Jacob's life as a whole, it seems to represent a *developmental ordeal.* This ordeal, a passage through conflict and pain inspired and directed by God, causes Jacob to slowly sacrifice his egocentric characteristics. It culminates in a reconciliation with his brother and his becoming "Israel," the embodiment of a unifying symbol for his people.

In the Old Testament story of Joseph and his brothers, we have another example of fraternal conflict focused around the issues of power and inheritance. Joseph begins this story as a spoiled and arrogant son. These characteristics bring him into conflict with his brothers, and the ensuing animosity begins another developmental ordeal. He is alienated from his family and his homeland, and matures through suffering to the point where the power situation is reversed. Having once been at the mercy of his brothers, they are now at his mercy, and he is in the position to save his people. He has gone from spoiled son to slave to wise and prudent counselor of the Pharaoh in a story reflecting the wisdom tradition of the Old Testament. Suffering, in these examples, is a means of coming to terms with our true selves, our destinies, and our relationship to God.

From another perspective, our suffering on other's behalf can show God's love. Rabbi Yehoshy'a ben Levi wrote: "He who accepts gladly the suffering of this world brings salvation to the world."[3] Transformation of the world is accomplished through the suffering of the individual prophet and the "suffering people." Once we have recognized our own responsibilities through our own suffering, we are faced with a new kind of suffering as we assume the burdens of others. This act endears us to a God who also suffers (and who also delights in the joy of his people), and so we participate in the growth and development of the world through this nobility.

This particular aspect of suffering may be considered a further differentiation of transcendent suffering. In relationship to this perspective in the ancient Jewish tradition, God also commanded the celebration of moments of splendid joy–a notion largely lost in the western Christian world in respect to the Old Testament tradition.

This transcendent suffering is shown best in the old Jewish tale of the Lamed-Vov.[4] The Lamed-Vov are 36 Just Men, secret saints, who through their deep caring and heartbreak, support the continued existence of the world. No one can tell them from other men and when one of them dies, another arises in order to maintain their number. Because their anguish over human suffering is so great that even God cannot comfort them, God allows the world of ordinary men to continue to exist. As an act of mercy toward them, "from time to time the Creator, blessed be His Name, sets forward the clock of the Last Judgment by one minute."[5]

Sheldon Kopp tells the story of:

> . . . a young boy whose aging grandfather informs him that the last Just Man has died without designating a successor. The boy is to take his place as one of the Lamed-Vov. He can soon expect to attain the glow that is the aura of his coming ascendancy. The boy is awed, but bewildered as to what he should do in this life as a Just Man. The old man assures him that he need only be himself, that he need not *do* anything to fulfill his destiny. In the meanwhile he need only continue to be a good little boy.
>
> But the child worries about his role, becoming obsessed with the idea that if he learns how to be a Just Man, perhaps God will be satisfied and spare his aging grandfather from dying. He fantasizes the grand self-tortures and self-sacrifices that may be required of him. Will he have to be dragged along the rough ground clinging to the tail of a Mongol pony, or would it be of greater merit if he were to be consumed by purifying flames while being burned at the stake?
>
> He is terrified, but ready to do whatever is required of him. He decides to work his way up, beginning by holding his breath as long as he can. When this does not seem enough, he holds a match to his hand, burning his palm to a painfully satisfying stigmatic char. His grandfather is deeply upset and yet touched, when he learns that the boy has been training himself to die in order to save the old man's life. He teaches the boy the nature of his monstrous error by explaining that as a Just Man, he will not be able to change anything. He will save no one. A Just Man need not pursue suffering. It will be there in the world for him as it is for each man. He need only be open to the suffering of others, knowing that he cannot change it. Without being able to save his brothers, he must let himself experience their pain, so that they need not suffer alone. This will change nothing for man, but it will make a difference to God.

> The boy wanders off trying to understand, but not seeing the sense or the worth of it all. His epiphany comes later that day when he catches a fly whose life he holds in the hollow of his hand. He knows a sudden sympathy for the terror and the trembling of the fly. The fly's anguish is suddenly his own as well. Releasing the fly from his own trembling hand, he suddenly feels the glow of becoming one of the Lamed-Vov. He has become one of the Just Men.[6]

However, the Judaic tradition does not simply advocate that we give in to suffering. Suffering is often dreadful, and we must fiercely question it and seek to understand it. First, we must examine ourselves carefully (Lam. 3,40). If we don't find the cause of our suffering in this examination, we must look next to see if we have been neglecting the Torah (law). If we cannot find the origins of our suffering there, it may be that our suffering is a result of love. The doctrine of the chastisement of love affirms that God gives special burdens to those who have a unique capacity to endure them and the righteous bear the burden of ascent. Once again, the burdens of ascent are the ordeals imposed upon chosen people to help purify them from their egocentric personalities in order that they may become more spiritual and closer to God.

It is frequently suggested that the wicked flourish because they are allowed to consume their rewards in this world. In fact, the doctrine of the resurrection was deduced from the justice of God to explain why the righteous suffer on this earth–to exhaust and thereby reduce whatever penalties they may have incurred. Cabalistic Judaism adopted the doctrine of reincarnation as an additional way to handle this problem. In this system, human souls are given repeated chances to atone in this world before the final judgment.

Jewish teaching acknowledges that, while we should try to avoid suffering where we can, there is a great deal of injustice in the world and a considerable amount of suffering is inflicted on the innocent. When it cannot be avoided, it must be accepted and endured. These teachings also point out that, while suffering is a part of this world, in the final analysis it is beyond human comprehension.

Christianity

As you might expect, many of the responses to suffering found in

Judaism are likewise found in Christian thought–for instance, suffering may be explained as the just payment for sin (Acts 5:1-11). However, the issue of suffering becomes more complicated in the *New Testament.* In John 9:3, Jesus rejects the notion of natural suffering being a result of sin, when he says that a man's blindness is caused neither by his own nor his parent's sin. Suffering also may serve a disciplinary, strengthening, and purifying function. "Suffering produces endurance, and endurance produces character, and character produces hope (Romans 5:3-4)." Such learning experiences are designed to help us literally conform to the image of Christ.

Another Christian interpretation of Jewish origin is that suffering is a characteristic of the burden of ascent.[7] Paul interprets his suffering as intrinsic to his missionary activity: "I only know that in every city the Holy Spirit warns me that prison and hardships are facing me (Acts 20:23)." Entire Christian communities were persecuted for their beliefs, and for them the experience of suffering was both inevitable and welcome, something to be confronted rather than avoided. "The Apostles left the Sanhedrin, rejoicing because they had been counted worthy of suffering disgrace for the Name (Acts 5:41; see also Second Corinthians 12:9–10 and Luke 22:42)." This attitude of welcoming persecution gladly sometimes reached the extreme of giving one's own life rather than transgressing God's commandments. Jesus embodied this principle when he became a martyr to his messianic mission.

In addition, Jesus represents the Gospel's idea of the suffering servant, one who suffers to spread God's word. The Gospel writers fuse this concept found in Isaiah 53, with that of the Messiah, God's anointed savior, to form a synthesis that was not present in the earlier scriptures. Jesus is depicted as the one whose suffering, crucifixion, and resurrection make him the symbol through whom human beings may hope for a similar spiritual destiny. The death and resurrection of Christ are bound together in the eternal cycle of transformation. Similarly, Christians are bound to the body of Christ and through this connection participate in the cycle of Christian transformation. "But now, by dying to what once bound us, we have been released from the law so that we serve in the new way of the Spirit, and not in the old way of the written code (Romans 7:6)." In this process, Christians are dead to the old realm of desperation and sin, released from the Law of Moses and introduced into the new transcendent realm of the Spirit.

Paul further developed the Christian concept of Christ's suffering. Christ's death not only combined a propitiatory sacrifice (which expiates sin and achieves forgiveness) and a paschal sacrifice (a vicarious sacrifice for all), but went beyond them and became a colossal cosmic occurrence. We can overcome the suffering of this world, in Paul's view, only by sharing in Christ's suffering, which also opens us to sharing his comfort. "For just as the sufferings of Christ flow into our lives, so also through Christ our comfort overflows (Second Corinthians 1:5)." Christ's suffering is not merely a historical fact but a continual reality—*eternally* renewed in the present. According to Paul, Christ *had* to be incarnated, to suffer crucifixion and be resurrected, in order for the individual to believe that his own suffering and death can be overcome through faith in a risen Christ.

Islam

Islam has sometimes been defined as "Judaism plus missionary endeavor, or Christianity minus Saint Paul." Mecca is the Holy City and center of Islam. Mohammed is the "Praised One," who had the revelation from Heaven that was then written in the Islamic holy book, the *Koran.*

The Islamic view is that suffering falls into two general categories. First, it can be a punishment for sin. This sort of suffering may be educational, directing one toward the true path, as well as punitive. Since disbelief is the greatest sin, the greatest suffering is considered to be the suffering of the soul of the unbeliever. In the second category, suffering is a trial of man's belief. This concept is based on the idea that the true Muslim will stand by his faith no matter how much he suffers.

Islam ascribes perfect justice to God. Evildoers will thus be punished in this world and also in the next. Furthermore, there will be a judgment day when the souls of good Muslims will be restored to dwell in a paradisiacal earth eternally. Sinners and unbelievers will be cast into Hell to be burned and tormented forever. Since the lack of belief is the root of evil in Islam, evil begins with man, and subsequently suffering as a punishment also originates with man. The suffering that tests the strength of a man's belief allows God to look into the innermost depth of his soul.

Yet the justice of God may not be apparent to humans, as this story from the 18th Book of the *Koran* shows.

> Khidr (or Kidher) the first angel of God has joined Moses in the desert. As they proceed, Khidr is afraid that Moses cannot witness what Khidr does without becoming angry. If Moses cannot trust Khidr and bear with him, Khidr will have to leave him. Soon Khidr scuttles the fishing boat of some poor villagers. Then, with Moses watching, he murders a young man. Finally, he restores the fallen wall of a city of unbelievers.
>
> Moses becomes angry and disgusted, and Khidr has to leave him. But before he goes, Khidr explains the purpose of his actions to Moses. Sinking the boat saved it for its owners. Pirates were on the way to steal it, and as it was, the fisherman could later salvage it. The young man was going to commit a heinous crime, and by killing him Khidr saved his pious parents from infamy. Khidr had preserved the treasure of two pious young men, saving them from ruin by restoring the wall they had hidden it under. Moses, too late, saw that his judgment had been shallow and that what had appeared to be evil, in fact was not.

Still, the Islamic tradition does not welcome suffering as a way of proving one's faith, as does Christianity. Neither is suffering something to be avoided whenever possible, as in Judaism. Suffering is considered a necessary component of life that should be alleviated when it can be, and endured when it can not. One should not loose hope or faith in God by surrendering to a fatalism, even while suffering.

Islam allows for both a passive and an active response to suffering. In the passive approach, we should accept suffering as God's will and a test of our belief in God and have faith that God will not force any soul beyond its capacity. In the active approach, we should not only endure our suffering but also perform good works and help ease the burdens of others. This will serve reciprocally to alleviate our own suffering by tipping the cosmic scales a little bit more in our direction.

Buddhist and Yoga Philosophy

The eastern approach to suffering, on the other hand, is radically different. The foundation of Buddhist teaching is the "Four Noble Truths" which Buddha expressed in his first discourse, the "Sermon at Benares." The first of these truths is that, "Everything is suffering" in the final analysis; existence by its nature is full of grief. We search for something stable and permanent, such as an inner self or immortal soul, only because we are ignorant and blind. All that we see of life in this world is transitory, according to Buddha. Our life is only a process made up of the ongoing emergence and disappearance of the elements of existence in a seeming continuum. Buddha preached in the Four Noble Truths that *desire* and the *attachment to life* are the origins of suffering for they keep the cycle of existence in motion.

We can obtain detachment from life by following the Holy Eightfold Path, extinguishing our suffering by abandoning desire, even the desire for life. This task is only possible if we recognize that everything–even if it is pleasant, important, and constant–is fleeting and, therefore, subject to suffering. If we can lose ourself in this way, we can face everything with serenity.

Psychologically, the cause of pain and suffering in the Buddhist system is that we assign an exaggerated importance to our ego existence because we cannot see that our ego is dependent on deeper things. The gateway to growth is to undermine our egocentric position by following the path of self-denial. The resulting void leads us beyond our personal perspective toward the goal of great compassion toward others. When our desire ends, we gain the wisdom to be free. This liberation leads to the undoing of all the foundations of existence resulting in extinction and, therefore, nirvana.

In the Yoga tradition, in which much of the essence of Oriental spirituality lies, pain is part of the law of existence and has a positive, stimulating value. Pain is a reminder that the only way to be free is to cast off the illusions of the world of phenomena and awaken to the true nature of spirit. The point of departure of yogic meditation is concentration on an object, a thought, or God. We cannot obtain this concentration on a single point if our body is in an uncomfortable position or if our respiration is out of rhythm, so the first goal of yoga is to bring our bodily functions under control, including our senses and thoughts.

However, Yoga practices go beyond simple control–they are the beginning of a process that binds the individual self to the absolute self, the union of Atman and Brahman. We can reach this union if we fulfill three conditions: a blameless moral life, self-discipline, and the control of bodily functions through certain postures. When we are able to fulfill these conditions and withdraw our senses from the external world, then we no longer notice what is going on around us.

Even in this brief discussion, it is clear that the Buddhist and Yogic traditions are difficult for Westerners to understand. While people in the Eastern traditions seek the condition of emptiness and imagelessness in order to free themselves from nature, Westerners look for who and what they are, even at the bottom of their greatest suffering. While Eastern religions say little about what God is (Brahman) or even what man is (Atman), we attempt to understand suffering in order to understand both man and God.

Still, even in Buddhism, suffering is both deserved and welcome. It is the consequence of misdeeds or mistakes committed in previous lives, and it is the only way to absorb and liquidate the karmic debt that each of us carries and to determine the cycle of future existence.

Conclusion

Of course, such a brief discussion is bound to overlook the various sects and denominations that derive from these three religions, not to mention the widely differing approaches to suffering held by the individuals in these groups. Yet our own struggles, though unique in many ways, contain the same conflicts, projections, and divisions that have been part of the human condition in an infinite variety for centuries.

These conflicts and the ways in which the various religions

deal with them show how difficult it is for humankind to live with the idea of divinity. The exploration of the nature of God plunges us into the paradoxes of life and shows us how little we understand it all. Yet the further we go, if we can stand it, the more we discover about ourselves, life, and God.

Revelation, whether from God or the unconscious, leads to both fascination and dread, so the collective ego in religions (what Jung called the "archetypal scribes and pharisees") quickly try to institutionalize the revelation and create an illusion of not only knowing the unknowable, but being able to bargain with it. In the same way, many psychologists try to reduce and concretize the manifestations of the unconscious, bringing them under the illusion of rational control. Or, they try to ignore the unknown altogether, focusing on cognition and behavior.

In discussing twentieth century man, Jung noted that "The one thing we refuse to admit is that we are dependent on powers that are beyond our control." He then continues:

> It is true, however, that in recent times civilized man has acquired a certain amount of will power, which he can apply where he pleases. He has learned to do his work efficiently without having recourse to chanting and drumming to hypnotize him into the state of doing. He can even dispense with a daily prayer for divine aid. He can carry out what he proposes to do, and he can apparently translate his ideas into action without a hitch, whereas the primitive seems to be hampered at each step by fears, superstitions, and other unseen obstacles to action. The motto "Where there's a will, there's a way" is the superstition of modern man.
>
> Yet in order to sustain his creed, contemporary man pays the price in a remarkable lack of introspection. He is blind to the fact that, with all his rationality and efficiency, he is possessed by "powers" that are beyond his control. His gods and demons have not disappeared at all; they have merely got new names. They keep him on the run with restlessness, vague apprehensions, psychological complications, an insatiable need for pills, alcohol, tobacco, food–and, above all, a large array of neuroses.[8]

The deep and numinous symbols we find in these religions call our psyche beyond our ego's inflation, rigidity, and narrow perspective. This call threatens the stability of our ego, confronting it with the incomprehensible and irrational. Isolation leads to panic, and panic leads to anxiety. Then we have a *Krisis*, a separation, the Greek root of the work crisis.

As this crisis develops the split between the conscious and unconscious grows wider. As the unconscious begins to insinuate itself into our decisions and its repressed images and symbols start to show up in our dreams and fantasies, we often wonder if we are losing our minds. After all, practical people living within their ego-reality often look at the mystics and others who have experienced great inner turmoil and transformation and consider them *crazy*.

This split is entirely different from the separation that the developing ego must make from the unconsciousness as our personal identity begins to form. In this later-life *Krisis,* the ego is finished with its earlier developmental differentiation from the unconscious. But, instead of reconnecting to the center of our personality, it has walled itself off from the inner world and in all likelihood, most of the outer. As Jung observed, all neurosis in the second half of life has a spiritual basis.

5

The Cosmic Pilgrimage: Jesus Christ and the Cross

The birth of Christ reorganized our historical perspective, becoming the center point in our concept of time. For Christians, Christ's birth is a new beginning in the relationship between humanity and God, connecting the ordinary world of practical or concrete *reality* to the *Eternal Reality* in which all lesser realities are contained. Time and eternity are thus joined and Christ's birth is an eternal event that finds its value as it is eternally lived in the human soul.

In *Answer to Job,* Jung suggests that previous mythological motifs, such as the general hero story, the dying god, and the son of a god, seemed to develop in a pattern leading to the birth of Christ. Earlier gods, such as the father god Zeus, were often numinous figures but had never become personalities. Zeus had little interest in relating to human beings and certainly didn't have any of the personality characteristics necessary to engage in personal relationships with humans. Yahweh on the other hand, seemed to have an endless fascination with his human creatures, but still remained distant, transcendent. What stands out clearly in the life of Christ is Christ's personal love of mankind. In Christian tradition, the liturgical year is based on the repetition of the Nativity, Passion, Death, and Resurrection, the events of

Christ's life that forever changed the relationship between God and man.

The life of Christ presents many parallels to the individuation process. Jung notes that "Individuation is a heroic and often tragic task, the most difficult of all, it involves suffering, a passion of the Ego."[1] When we follow our individuation process, we may discover that the reason for our suffering is unique. Searching for the meaning of our suffering is equivalent to searching for the meaning of our lives.

Animals live and die in an instinctual way. If we are not connected to something greater than ourselves, we may do the same to a large extent. But because we are more conscious than animals, we suffer more than they do, especially in the realm of the psyche. And we are the only creatures who encounter the paradox of suffering–suffering can produce strength, wisdom, love, and compassion, and the growth of consciousness–even while we are longing to be free of our pain.

In this respect Jung pointed out that the symbolism of the Mass repeats the whole drama of the incarnation.

> Looked at from the psychological standpoint, Christ, as the Original Man (Son of Man, second Adam . . .), represents a totality which surpasses and includes the ordinary man, and which corresponds to the total personality that transcends consciousness. We have called this personality the 'self' . . . the mystery of the Eucharist transforms the soul of the empirical man, who is only a part of himself, into his totality, symbolically expressed by Christ. In this sense, therefore, we can speak of the Mass as the *rite of the individuation process.*[2]

While all men suffer, a *healer* not only suffers but also finds a way to surmount his sufferings. Mystics experience the immanence of God (psychologically the archetype of the Self), and several have shown suffering as the central metaphor of Christianity by expressing the stigmata. Healers in other traditions, from Chiron to modern psychoanalysts, have carried their wounds, transformed them to *sacred wounds,* and then used them as the basis for healing others. Jesus is an excellent example of this process as he suffered, died, and surmounted death through his resurrection. Theologically, he is considered to have done this for us. Psychologically, Christ does not do it for us, but calls on each of us to take personal responsibility for growing to the same state of consciousness that Jesus himself demonstrated.

Christ is both man and God. As man, he was born and lived a concrete, personal, and unique life. As God, he is the "King of Kings," "the Anointed One": "You are from below; I am from above. You are of this world; I am not of this world (John 8:23)." His life is an example of wisdom, knowledge, and intelligence that amazed those around him. The miracles of Jesus flowed from the creative and saving Spirit of God. He was given the Spirit at his baptism where "the Holy Spirit descended on him in bodily form like a dove (Luke 3:21)." We might remember that the dove also symbolized the ancient goddess of love, giving further emphasis to the importance of love in Christ's mission.

Finally, in the Garden of Gethsemane, sweating blood before his crucifixion and with the Spirit of God departing from him, Christ faced his passion and death in his full humanity, that is, saturated in the blood and guts of life. Hans Küng[3] noted that Jesus was "the image of *the sufferer pure and simple.*" This suffering is not to be understood as despair, "but as an act of supreme self-sacrifice, of ultimate love for God and men." Küng points out that Christ "is a sufferer who does not exude compassion, but demands it himself; who does not rest within himself, but totally gives himself."

In this, Christ differs from Buddha, the Compassionate One, as well as from the other significant figures in world religions. Christ came to be crucified in order to evoke in our hearts compassion for the suffering of life, to turn our egos from blind engagement with the values of this world to a deeper spiritual life. "It is in compassion with Christ that we turn to Christ, and the injured one becomes our Savior."[4] This theme also appears in the figure of the Fisher King in the Grail legends, the injured one who becomes the savior because his suffering calls forth the courage and humanity of the human heart. As we respond to this suffering, we reach a state of oneness with God. The material world is not to be rejected nor despised, nor is it to be *idealized*–it is to be made sacred as it bears the life and creativity of God.

An example of Christ's dual nature can do more than bring meaning to our suffering. His life is a model of the integration of our conscious and unconscious minds. By following this model, we can realize his wholeness within ourselves. Psychologically, we can understand Christ's double nature as the two different values in ourselves; spirit and matter uniting in Christ as a dual symbol for both the individuating ego and the Self. Suffering, then, leads us to God, to the Self, and to our own inner unity. Redemption corresponds to the union of opposites through grace.

Normally when we face contradictions or paradoxical situations in life we feel tension, frustration, depression, and anxiety. We learn early on to cope with these feelings by unconsciously repressing one side of the conflict or the other and adopting an ideal that justifies this position. For example, you may remember the depressed woman we discussed in Chapter One. Her mother had died when she was an adolescent and her non-expressive father had coped by working hard, doing his duty, and providing for the family. As a young girl, she adopted his attitude as her ideal and became non-expressive, hard working, and outwardly tough at the expensive of denying her entire emotional nature. Eventually, this denial caught up with her as a major depression.

As in this case, we generally find that these conflicts and others such as the conflict between societal values and personal fulfillment continue and we have to keep dealing with them. We may do so by rigidifying our ideal or taking a cynical, depressive, victimized position. If we do, we're inviting some form of neurotic suffering and will generally end up inflicting it on those close to us as well as ourselves.

On the other hand, we can struggle to know more fully what we are doing, to face both the affirmation and the negation, often desire and obligation, that we are caught between. Knowing both conflicting polarities and holding the tension between them may seem like a denial of life and certainly involves suffering. But this conscious position opens us to our own center and allows a third position, that we could not have previously imagined, to emerge. Both prayer and dreams can open this connection to our center and help us evolve neurotic suffering into true suffering and both true suffering and developmental suffering into transcendent suffering.

A man I once counseled was stuck between finding a new

career and his obligations to his family. While in therapy, he dreamed of a lion living deep in the jungle foliage. He realized that the lion is a powerful symbol of a kind of energy–a strength, vitality, courage, power, dignity, and ability to fight–that he had lost touch with in his own nature. (In the *Narnia Tales*, C.S. Lewis presents Christ as the lion Aslan, both a ruling and a redemptive figure.) The man knew that it would take courage, strength, and the willingness to fight in order to make his move. He also knew that he could do so with dignity and the support of his own nature. He experienced a new sense of inner unity and security.

The story of Christ's life and teachings amplifies many of the points we are discussing. As we know, Christ was not born into the grand style. He was born poor, in a manger, close to the earth and the animals–close to instinctual life. From this beginning and throughout his ministry, he pointed out how power and success are both important and also dangerous to spiritual development. His birth also demonstrated the dignity of poverty, weakness, and suffering. Poverty of the spirit, *humility* (from the word *humus* meaning the quality of the soil), brings us to the quiet state of receptivity in which the seeds of the spirit may flourish. The glory and simplicity of his birth are seen in the attendance of the angels, the three wise men, and the shepherds.

Immediately after his birth, we read of the escape to Egypt and the slaughter of the innocents by King Herod the Great. In psychological terms, if we are going to develop consciousness, spiritual renewal, and psychological growth, we also must be willing to endure the slaughter of our naive, innocent attitudes. We also must protect our beginning individuation from the wrath of social conventions and expectations. These internalized conventions originally form our development, but at a certain point in our growth they turn negative and fill us with fear and anxiety. If we constantly ask ourselves "What will people think?" "What do people expect?" "Will my spouse, parents, children, or boss be upset?" we are imprisoned by our conventions.

Like Christ's birth, the baptism in the River Jordan (with water and spirit) represents the new and growing connection with the Self, but the temptations in the desert that immediately follow (Luke 4:1–13) show the other side of the coin–the almost irresistible temptation to inflation and the danger that the individuating ego might be completely swallowed by the unconscious. We must remember that we cannot become fully conscious without dealing with these temptations. They help us establish reasonable boundaries to our ego, and at the same time give it the ground in our personality to stand on.

In the first temptation, the devil invites Christ to turn stones into bread. Psychologically, this temptation represents an effort to put the Self at the service of our ego. This temptation is often encountered in psychology under the guise of "self-actualization," where we make economic and emotional security a goal in our life rather than have it be a result of our individuation process. We end up seeking a shallow psychological well-being rather than looking for a deeper source of spiritual nourishment.

In the next temptation, the devil takes Jesus to the top of a mountain and shows him the splendors of all the kingdoms of the earth. The devil then says to Jesus that if he will bow down and worship the devil Jesus can have all of these glories. This temptation represents the confrontation with our egocentric ambition for power, control, and success, and the inflation of considering as "personal" the power that actually belongs to the Self and life. Jesus also refuses this path to political power.

In the third and final temptation, the devil takes Jesus to Jerusalem, the spiritual center of the world. From the highest point on the temple, he suggests that Jesus prove his divine nature by throwing himself down since the angels would catch him and bear him up. This final temptation shows us how easy it is to become spiritually inflated. Often when we are successful, we are tempted to forget our mortality and our humanity. Our society also urges us to constantly push ourselves beyond our limits, causing us to be less and less present and responsible in truly human ways. People who pursue spiritual and psychological journeys also fall prey to this temptation by losing touch with the concerns of the flesh and the earth.

These temptations remind us that following our own path is as difficult as walking a tight rope. At any point, we are in danger of falling over and being swept away in a torrent of worldly passion. We must avoid the temptation to usurp the energy of the Self for the purposes of the ego–materialism, power, and spiritual grandiosity. The temptations are always there, testing our commitment to the call of being a servant-messiah to the Self. Suffering through this struggle strengthens our character and deepens our relationship to the Self and to life.

Handled correctly, the confrontation between the ego and the Self can lead to a dialectical relationship between the two. In such a case, the ego experiences its own autonomy, possibilities, and limits, yet recognizes its dependence on the higher entity of the Self. This paradoxical balance does not imply a denial of the ego, for if the ego is denied, there cannot be a nourishing, loving connection between the ego and the Self. The ego has to be aware of its own values and develop its own possibilities. We can see this in the parable of the talents (Matthew 25:14) where all the capacities, intelligence, and abilities of the disciples have to be used in order to multiply. They can't be buried, simply hoarded and retained.

If we turn to the Sermon on the Mount (Matthew 5–7), we find our normal social aspirations flipped upside down–as when we are told to love our enemies or to fast cheerfully. However, if we pursue these paradoxes, we stand to recover values that we may have neglected. "Seen in this light Jesus's teachings become a kind of manual for promoting the individuation process."[5] To further illustrate this point, we would like to consider eight of the most familiar paradoxes of the Sermon on the Mount: the Beatitudes.

"Blessed are the poor in spirit, for theirs is the kingdom of heaven." Becoming aware of our emptiness of spirit, the lack of meaning in our lives is the best and indeed only way to become receptive to what we need. This receptivity opens us to the unconscious and the Self, the experience of God and "the kingdom within."

"Blessed are those who mourn, for they will be comforted." It is better to accept suffering than to reject it and, thereby, lose contact with our own nature. For as we deny and repress characteristics during our development, we tend to "project" these characteristics onto other people. Any unusually strong feeling of liking or disliking, despising or admiring someone is generally a sign of projection. Projections make relationships difficult because we are dealing with self-created illusions rather than the actual other person. Taking our projections back and owning the characteristics as our own is a painful process whether the characteristics are good or bad. If they are bad, we don't enjoy admitting them about ourselves. If they are good, it hurts to realize that we have been disassociated from some of our best traits. In either case, mourning is called for.

We must recognize and abandon these projections in others in order to assimilate their content within our own personalities. As we do this, we lose the people around us as we knew them, and this loss is also painful. However, this loss is a prelude to the rediscovery of the world as it really is. The experience and acceptance of suffering, expressed by mourning, is the humble prerequisite for this transformation. As Edward Edinger writes, "Therefore mourners are fortunate because they are involved in a growth process. They will be comforted when the last projected value has been recovered in the psyche."[6]

"Blessed are the meek, for they will inherit the earth." The ego must maintain an attitude toward the Self that is receptive as well as submissive. In such a case, we are open to connect to the wholeness of our nature and the wholeness of life in new and unforeseeable ways.

"Blessed are those who hunger and thirst for righteousness, [or "justice"] for they will be filled." As is frequently the case in the Western tradition, we have the tendency to interpret this passage literally, as in Luke's version ("Blessed are those who hunger now, for they will be filled.") Far better to consider this passage as a metaphor for our spirituality, which needs to be nourished constantly, day by day, to satisfy for our inner guiding principles of right and justice. There are also the disenfranchised aspects of our psyche, now living in our shadow, that ask for justice, consideration, and attention, rather than expulsion, projection, or ignorance.

"Blessed are the merciful, for they will be shown mercy." It is a psychological principle that people who are most critical of others are, at a deep inner level, tortuously critical of themselves. Our unconscious projects our attitude toward it, and life reflects this attitude back at us once again. This relationship shows how important it is for the ego to develop a merciful attitude toward the unconscious, so it can provide, in its turn, openness and support to the ego. Mercy often needs to be balanced by justice, and both attitudes require that we have a highly differentiated personality. Otherwise, we can easily fall into naive sentimentalism or blind obedience to a so-called higher power.

"Blessed are the pure in heart, for they will see God." If our ego is relatively uncontaminated by unconscious identifications and projections, and if it is honest and self-reflecting, then it will be open to encounter and relate to the Self.

"Blessed are the peacemakers, for they shall be called sons of God." Our function of the ego is to mediate between the different aspects of the psyche. This task brings together the totality of the psyche and lets us realize the divinity in our own humanity. But we must be careful of two pitfalls in this process. If our ego identifies with only one side in a psychic conflict, we will end up with a rift in our personality, rather than taking a step toward wholeness. Also, if we repress or deny part of our psyche in an effort to achieve the appearance of "harmony," we are really creating potential psychic volcanoes.

"Blessed are those who are persecuted for righteousness' sake, for theirs is the kingdom of heaven." The ego must be able to endure suffering without giving in to bitterness and resentment in order to maintain a relationship to the psyche. The reward for this endurance is contact with the life-giving and life-enriching images of the inner depths.

Jesus delivers this paradoxical discourse as the Son of God whose authority is greater than that of any social or religious institution. Psychologically, the Sermon on the Mount reflects the same authority, that of the Self, the image of God within. Jesus continually reveals the texture of the Eternal hidden in the ordinary and living in the present. Thus, we are faced with radical truths in the original sense that they go to the very roots of life. In this sense, the Beatitudes, rather than happening at the end of time, may be fulfilled now by those who partake in the individuation process shown in the life and teachings of Jesus.

It is most important to understand that these sayings are realized by being lived. They are not a set of values or guidelines to be followed in order to live a more spiritual life. In fact, to reduce them to such a concrete level is to succumb to the third temptation of Christ. In such a case we are trying to become spiritual without going through the necessary human process of development, a sure road to spiritual inflation, a loss of the values of the human heart and, in the end, to spiritual failure. We simply cannot transform our ego simply by observing the Law (Matthew 5:21) or by a sterile obedience to a path developed for us, be it spiritual or psychological.

In the Grail legend, each knight began his search for the Grail (the container of the blood of Christ, the vitality of life) by entering the forest at a point where it was darkest and there was no path. And each did so alone because they thought it would be a disgrace to go in a group.[7] This lonely quest, like the lonely journey of Jesus, shows one of the central values of Western man–the fulfillment of the character of the individual. We must earn our character, bringing it forth from the potential within ourselves, grounding it in our own natures, assimilating it into our living experience. This is a far different notion from those of the East, where one is to lose one's individual character by following a way that has already been worked out by a teacher.

The first step in this character-building process is for our ego to become aware of its own existence and position. It must differentiate itself from the unconscious, where it begins as the member of a "crowd." This happens to some extent for everyone in childhood, but if the process is incomplete or flawed, we have a hard time being our own master. Someone with an incomplete ego finds it easy to follow collective patterns, projecting their shadows onto others. We can see an example of such a collective approach to life in the story of the woman caught in adultery (John, 8:1–11). The community was ready to stone her because it projected part of its own psychology (the "adulterer," the instinctual) onto her. Christ's approach was to take the townspeople from the collective to the personal level ("If *any one of you* is without sin, let him be the first to throw a stone at her") so that they might become more conscious and move toward individuation by becoming aware of new unknown parts of ourselves. In our era, we can see in the cases of divorce, homosexuality, and abortion what a difficult time religious institutions, and we ourselves, have in moving from a one-sided collective position to a personal one based on our human culpability.

Many people in recent times are growing disillusioned with "individualism" and are urging a new search for community. These people frequently cannot understand the need for individuality in the individuation process as well as in the community. Jung maintained that for a community to function in a healthy manner, it must be a community of individuals–because to be truly responsible we must be connected to our own center. If we don't know who we are in the deeper sense, then we are vulnerable to developing an undifferentiated dedication to collective ideals and principles. Such an undifferentiated dedication to ideals, no matter how *good* they seem, is idolatry in a much more subtle and dangerous manner than the worship of "graven images." Such one-sided people often create painful and divisive situations, from the enabling spouse who drives a mate into alcoholic rage, to the militant anti-abortionist who harasses doctors, to the self–made martyr who supports "good" so strenuously that he only succeeds in annoying others. Tragically such people are often searching in a desperate, neurotic manner for their own existence as a person. Many even resort to neurotic self-mutilation to feel that they are alive in their own bodies.

The parable of the Prodigal Son (Luke 15:11–32) is an example of this experience. The story begins with the younger of two sons who, because he is not aware of his fortunate position in life, must go through a long, difficult journey. First, he loses the support of his wealthy family and his relationship to his father. Then he must realize through suffering and emptiness that he has lost the values of his life. Once he has developed a more humble attitude, he finds himself back in his previous position, but with a renewed sense of solidarity to his personality. His older, less passionate, and more dutiful brother, on the other hand, has sheltered himself from the risk of struggle and is left confused and envious because he has no real knowledge of life. He cannot understand either his brother's individuation or his father's true compassion.

Throughout the gospels, Jesus performs miracles that alleviate suffering. These miracles fall in three basic categories:[8] exorcism, physical healing, and nature miracles. These miracles were never performed simply for display; when they were demanded as a sign (Mark 8:11–13) or for selfish or frivolous reasons (Matthew 4:1–7), Jesus refused. The miracles were performed in order to provide individuals with unique personal experiences of renewal. He performed them in a spirit of benevolence and compassion.

The miracles take us beyond the world of common sense consciousness and into the world of the supernatural. In this world, as Jung pointed out, it is in our faults, our illnesses, and our deformities that our salvation lies. Where we are wounded and where we have stumbled is where we will find the psychological gold that holds the key to our new development and renewal. Balance comes from leaning on our faults, amplifying and understanding them, as they can connect us to the Self, the image of God within.

The miracles stand as a sign of Jesus's love and compassion but also as a reminder of how important it is not to be too concerned with worldly things. Christ wants us to turn our minds to the reality of the spirit, in a conscious manner–a manner that reflects that we know what we are doing and are not blindly following rules. The *spirit* exists, even if we can't fit it into the Cartesian coordinates of a system of clear and distinct ideas. And as the incarnation of Christ shows, we must develop an understanding of the world that includes God in both spirit and matter.

Twentieth century man seems to have had trouble anthropomorphizing God, of giving God personal attributes. This anthropomorphizing (which is actually supported by centuries of religious tradition) lets us *personalize* our relationship to God in a way that we sometimes "personify" and dialogue with figures in our psyche–a technique that often helps the people we work with. If we simply relate to our Self or God as an amorphous "higher power," then we have little chance of feeling personally related to anything transcendent.

As with dream figures, we must be careful that in personifying God we do not mistake our personification for the totality of God–to take our personification literally. There is always the mystery of the Self beyond our understanding of it and likewise the mystery of God represents what we can never fully know. Only the symbolic images can connect us with either.

We have a good example of taking God too literally in John 6:1–15, where the people saw the powerful things Jesus was able to perform (like feeding the five thousand) and wanted him to become their literal king. We often see a similar *literal* attitude in analysis, when an analysand says, "Just tell me what to do," treating their troubles like spot-removal rather than looking at the underlying psychic issues. This attitude, in both religion and analysis, also includes a surrender of responsibility–such literalists ask either God or their analyst to make their decisions for them. Such literalists may also tend to rationalize their way into shallow and temporary solutions to suffering rather than struggling on to find the spiritual kingdom within themselves.

If we are in a psychological crisis, either neurotic, developmental, or as the result of a natural tragedy, we find it easy to lose our perspective and surrender to panic and despair, the way the disciples did in the storm while Jesus slept on the boat to Bethsaida (John 6:45). When there is too much pain, it is easy to lose sight of our healing center and be overcome by fear and anxiety. As we grow from stage to stage in life, we encounter a developmental "storm" during each transition. Depending on our circumstances, they may be mild or they may be extremely turbulent, dark, and threatening. As we move from the sheltered world of childhood into adolescence and the great unknown of sexuality, our developing ego may feel like a little boat on a stormy sea. And the passage to self-responsibility and maturity is never easy and often leaves scars and even open wounds. Then if we continue our growth until we begin developing our true being as individuals, we find suffering and turbulence again as we separate from the values of our parents and social institutions.

Of course, we can avoid this entire problem by never paying attention to anything beyond the values of our "world parents" (practical, conventional wisdom). The Old Testament laws as summarized in the Ten Commandments (especially the fourth, "Honor thy father and mother") are a good instance of such a conventional system. From a psychological perspective, we must remember that the Old Testament sort of system is designed to help us conform to society, the path we follow in the first half of life. But if we interpret and follow these commandments blindly, we may find ourselves captured within the legal framework of the Old Testament.

For a young adolescent, a developing individual, or a developing society, the teachings of the Old Testament provide the necessary structure for building an identity and civilizing the instincts. But as we move into the second half of life, toward psychological and spiritual maturity, we should start to consider the New Testament as a model, for developing a higher level of consciousness. Sometimes this may involve a *necessary sin* that turns our lives upside down, shocking our spouses, parents, friends and coworkers. When the depressed woman in Chapter One decided to confront her father, she was violating the notion of honoring her father and mother in the eyes of her siblings and even in her own.

Jesus taught more about this transformation when he compared himself to a sword separating father and son, mother and daughter (Matthew 10:34–36) and when he refers to higher symbolic relationships as more authentic than the ties of blood (Matthew 12:48–50). In perhaps his best example, Luke 13:32–33, he refers to Herod as a "fox," replying fearlessly to Herod's hostility with determination and courage. Herod was a king who had lost both his nobility and his capacity to rule–his only interest was in power and self-preservation. Christ's Herod, a descendent of the Herod of the slaughter of the innocents, represents the worst side of parental and cultural values that have become concrete and institutionalized. The depressed woman in our case had to cut through crippled attitudes to reach her own authenticity and to open her life to reconciliation and renewal.

It is simple to see from all this that the development of consciousness, the coming of light, also brings with it suffering and a sense of loneliness. It was probably in this mood that Jesus withdrew from Galilee for a period of reflection in order to strengthen and renew himself (Mark 7:24). It also appears from the harshness of his words (Mark 7:27 and Matthew 15:24) that he was feeling some tension. And it was after this retreat that he began to teach that the "Son of Man must suffer" (Mark 8:31).

In light of what follows in the gospel story, we may conclude that, during his retreat and reflection, Jesus found a solution that enabled him to return to his disciples and the world. It may not be entirely fanciful to suppose that when he later said to the deaf mute "Be opened" (Mark 7:34) and to the blind man "Do you see anything?" (Mark 8:23), that he was thinking of his disciples and perhaps even of himself.

Such a level of consciousness, where our eyes and ears are really open to hear and see through our concrete reality, can sometimes be seen and attained in analysis. Usually it comes only after a difficult period of incubation on the part of the analysand. But if the analyst has done his or her own inner work, the analyst may be able to trigger the shift to the next level in the analysand. Analysts who have not done their own inner work may also destroy this possibility, at least temporarily, for their analysands.

In the film, *A Matter of Heart,* Mary Bancroft reported that C.G. Jung used such an "ear opening" intervention with her. She tells how she asked him "Why is everybody in the world so mean to me?" Jung shot back, "Why are you so mean to everybody in the world?" This objection provoked such a violent reaction in her that it was only after a year (and a nasty letter to Jung) that she was able to see how blind she had been and resumed her analysis.

Bancroft responded so angrily because she was dealing with a rather difficult subject: her shadow. The shadow, as we have seen, includes the negative attributes we would prefer to hide, and that we would like to think are only at work in the lives of our enemies. And so we project these qualities onto others while our ego lives in its illusory and rigid world. In *Aion,* Jung wrote:

> It is often tragic to see how blatantly a man bungles his own life and the life of others yet remains totally incapable of seeing how much the whole tragedy originates in himself, and how he continually feeds it and keeps it going. Not consciously, of course–for consciously he is engaged in bewailing and cursing a faithless world that recedes further and further into the distance. Rather, it is an unconscious factor which spins the illusions that veil his world. And what is being spun is a cocoon, which in the end will completely envelop him."[9]

If we have the courage to search out, face, and accept the qualities of our shadow into our consciousness, then our ego will not only become more stable, but we can use the creativity and dynamic energy–the good qualities–that have been hidden in the shadow. Jesus clearly suggested this paradoxical truth when he said "Love your enemies and pray for those who persecute you" (Matthew 5:44) and "Settle matters quickly with your adversary who is taking you to court" (Matthew 5:25). Also, in the parable of the Good Samaritan (Luke 10:25–37), the unfortunate man is rescued by a dishonored stranger who, we could imagine, is the positive aspect of his shadow.

It may help to recast this parable in more modern terms. The victim, who has been beaten, stripped, and robbed, is our ego, our sense of conscious identity. While we make our journey from the center (Jerusalem) into life (Jerico), we have perhaps been battered and robbed by a culture driven by fear and desire. We are in the ditch, beaten and vulnerable. Who can help us? First our priest, minister, or rabbi comes by–and keeps going. Then perhaps our favorite college professor, counselor, or therapist. They keep going as well. Who comes next and stops to help us? Yassar Arafat. Yes, that is correct–Yassar Arafat.

Christ's parable turns our normal rational world upside down, bringing our projections crashing down on our heads. When we can consider one of our most despicable enemies nurturing and caring for us when we are vulnerable, we have some idea of what getting in touch with our shadow really means. Perhaps considering this parable could help us find within ourselves the passionate religious fervor of the Middle East. Perhaps then we could enter the Grail castle as Parzival did, reconciled with Feirefiz, his dark brother from that mystical, violent land.

But before we can accept the positive side of our shadow, we have to deal with the negative side, the emotional, destructive, autonomous, and evil side. Because these negative shadow qualities are shared by a large number of people, they can display a terrifying magnetic force when we're still unconscious of them. This force is behind the mob mentality that will follow an irrational path with the force of an avalanche.[10]

> 'Crucify him,' they shouted. 'Why? What crime has he committed?' asked Pilate. But they shouted all the louder, 'Crucify him' (Mark 15:13–14).

The ego stands alone, facing the task of domesticating and transforming the blind power of the unconscious into something conscious. The same crowd that is so enthusiastic about him and wants him to be a king is now shouting "Crucify him!" when they find out that he is not going to make a kingdom in this world and share it with them. Also, the Scribes and Pharisees (the guardians of the cultural canons) lead the crowd against Jesus (Mark 12:28–34). Jesus has followed his own nature and so become more and more separated from the unconscious societal norms. Because of this, the Scribes and the Pharisees almost have to look at him as a false prophet, a "disturber of the status quo."[11]

We cannot live an authentic life without carrying a certain amount of guilt for violating some collective canon. In effect, the collective shadow responds to our independence in its own crude, impersonal, and wild way, as a backlash to the claims of the ego. Dealing with this mob means dealing with our unconscious relationship to the world parents, the parental aspects of social institutions, because it is the world parents who stir up the collective shadow, just as the Pharisees led the mob against Jesus. We can see how Christ dealt with the world parents in the gospel of Matthew:

> – The teachers of the Law and Pharisees sit in Moses's seat. So you must obey them and do everything they tell you. But do not do what they do, for they do not practice what they preach. (23:12)
>
> – Woe to you, blind guides. (23:16)
>
> – Woe to you, teachers of the Law and Pharisees, you hypocrites! You are like whitewashed tombs, which look beautiful on the outside but on the inside are full of dead men's bones and everything unclean. In the same way, on the outside you appear to people as righteous, but on the inside you are full of hypocrisy and wickedness. (23:27–28)

No wonder the collective shadow became murderous.

This conflict between an individual trying to live an authentic lie and the world parents is behind much of the suffering involved in the separation process. We can see this conflict between the individual life truly lived coming into conflict with the world parents on several different levels. We've already noted the conflict the depressed woman had over confronting her father. In Chapter

Three we saw, in the case of the physician changing careers in order to live a life truer to his nature, how conflict evolved halfway through his transformation. He was unable to meet the financial ideals he had regarding his family in his former life. These ideals were based on an upper middle-class value system that emphasized an affluent standard of living including expensive private schools and colleges. For a while he left his course of transformation and returned to a job that began destroying him. In his analysis, he came to grips with the fact that to live he must resume his course of change, reduce his family's standard of living, face their anger, and suffer the guilt of failing his former ideals.

In the case of catastrophic illnesses, we pointed out in Chapter One that our society expects the ill person to get back to his or her old self as quickly as possible and with a positive attitude in order to reduce the time that the rest of us are faced with the true reality of life.

The unique example of the separation and loneliness is given in Christ's experience in the Garden of Gethsemane, where his soul is "overwhelmed with sorrow to the point of death" (Matthew 26:38). There, as a human being, he faces the horror of his Passion and death, going through the "dark night of the soul."[12] In the end, he accepts the journey to Calvary in his full humanity crying, "My father, if it is not possible for this cup to be taken away unless I drink it, may your will be done" (Matthew 26:42).

From the gospels, we know that he spoke seven times while on the cross:

- Woman, behold your son. (John 19:26)
- Behold your mother. (John 19:26)
- I am thirsty. (John 19:28)
- It is finished. (John 19:30)
- Father forgive them for they know not what they do. (Luke 23:34)
- Truly I say to you, today you will be with me in Paradise. (Luke 23:43)
- My God, my God, why have you forsaken me? (Mark 15:34)

These sentences show that Jesus approached death, not as physical destruction, but as psychological completion. His death reflects a love of God as well as a compassion toward man. Christ's sacrifice results in the reconciliation of man (the body) and God (the image of the Self) and, in this sense, becomes the ultimate act of love.

The message of completion in Christ's final sayings is expressed on several different levels. We can associate the seven sayings with the seven days of creation, as if Christ's death were a seal upon the cosmos. Also the first of these seven sentences is directed to his mother and the last addresses his father showing that the cycle of growth is complete. His final lament is actually a quotation from the Old Testament, Psalm 22:1. By using this ancient lament, he is not giving a simple cry of desperation but is feeling the full weight of human misery, not as judgment but as an acceptance of the completion of the cycle of life.

He died with the sun of the past year on Good Friday, after the first full moon following the vernal solstice. He was resurrected with the new sun on Sunday, Easter Day, with the dawning of the spring equinox. Here again, there is a death to the old life and the rebirth to new, as nature and spirit parallel each other symbolically in the eternal dance.

The drama of this transformation in human life is also shown when, after his death, "the curtain of the temple was torn in two from top to bottom" (Mark 15:38). The separation between God and humankind was annulled, opening a new and living way to God. Psychologically, this models the opening of a new and more vital relationship with the Self.

There is an interesting passage from the Acts of John, an apocryphal text, where Christ institutes a mystical "round dance" while he is awaiting his arrest before his crucifixion. We can imagine the fear and confusion his disciples must have felt at the time, yet Jesus gathers them together to dance and sing hymns of praise to God. This act prepares them, spiritually and psychologically, for his journey toward his destiny.

In the dance, the disciples hold hands and form a circle while Jesus stands in the center, singing a song of praise. By taking part in a living mandala (the eternal symbol of wholeness and unity), each one of the twelve is connected with the center, Jesus, which soothes the confusion in the conscious realm. This is a beautiful example of how the relationship between the ego and Self works, where the singular takes part in the totality that transcends consciousness.

I will be saved and I will save, Amen.
I will be loosed and I will loose, Amen.
I will be wounded and I will wound, Amen.
I will be begotten and I will beget, Amen.
I will eat and I will be eaten, Amen.

I will be thought, being wholly spirit, Amen.
I will be washed and I will wash, Amen.
Grace paces the round. I will blow the pipe. Dance the round all, Amen.

The Eight [ogdoad] sings praises with us, Amen.
The Twelve paces the round aloft, Amen.
To each and all it is given to dance, Amen.
Who joins not the dance mistakes the event, Amen.

I will be united and I will unite, Amen.

A lamp am I to you that perceive me, Amen.
A mirror am I to you that know me, Amen.
A door am I to you that knock on me, Amen.
A way am I to you the wayfarer.

Now as you respond to my dancing, behold yourself in me who speaks . . . As you dance, ponder what I do, for yours is this human suffering which I will suffer. For you would be powerless to understand your suffering had I not been sent to you as the Logos by the Father . . . If you had understood suffering, you would have non-suffering. Learn to suffer, and you shall understand how not to suffer . . . Understand the Word of Wisdom in Me."[13]

Dancing through this dramatic moment is a way to establish the relationship between earth and sky, as a call for the descent of grace. By referring to the living center, each one of the twelve can:

. . . see himself in the reflecting centre, and his suffering is

> the suffering which the One who stands in the centre 'wills to suffer' . . . As the text says, you would not be able to understand what you suffer unless there were that Archimedean point outside, the objective standpoint of the self, from which the ego can be seen as a phenomenon. Without the objectivization of the self the ego would remain caught in hopeless subjectivity and would only gyrate round itself. But if you can see and understand your suffering without being subjectively involved, then, because of your altered standpoint, you also understand 'how not to suffer,' for you have reached a place beyond all involvements ('you have me as a bed, rest upon me').[14]

When we relate to the living, transcendental center, we do not see something different, but we can see what is already there differently.

More commonly to the Christian tradition than the mysticism of the dance is the mysticism of the cross. Even though the cross has a special meaning in the Christian tradition, it might be well to look at the variety of symbolic meanings it has had outside the Christian perspective as well. The cross is a primary symbol that relates three other fundamental symbols: the center, the square, and the circle. The intersection of its two straight lines coincides with the center and opens the center up to the outside. The cross additionally divides the circle into four parts and engenders the square. It is thus a symbol of union, where the four become one, and at the same time a symbol of dismemberment, where the one becomes four.

The cross also symbolizes the totality of space and time, with its center marking the meeting of four directions and then transcending them. The cross is compared to a tree, the mediator between earth and sky, representing the tension point of the union of opposites. It evokes verticality, and provides access to the invisible. It is the mythological threshold between time and eternity, the *axis mundi* (the world axis) through which heaven descends toward man. It is also the world–a tree that the shaman goes up to reach the top of the universe.

The four points of the cross recall the four cardinal points, the four winds, the four seasons of the year, the four rivers of Paradise in the garden of Eden, the four parts of a plant (root, stem, flower, and fruit), the four celestial beings (sky, sun, moon, and stars), and the four kinds of animals (those that crawl, those that fly, quadrupeds, and bipeds). The technique of weaving is cross-like, requiring two threads to cross at a center and transforming chaos into cosmos. Often the weaving art has been used to represent the concept of fate.

But within the historic Christian tradition, the cross was used as an instrument of torture and death. The protracted, ex*cruc*iating suffering that the cross inflicted and the extreme ignominy of this manner of execution led the Romans to consider the cross as the supreme penalty, the most wretched of deaths, generally reserved for the lowest classes. In fact, for several centuries the pagans of the empire were unable to understand the contradiction of a crucified god who, by so dying, becomes a saviour. Christians were accused of madness for daring to put a crucified man in the same place as the creator of the world and the master of the universe.

So it was not until the fifth century that images of Jesus on the cross begin to appear. But after that, crosses were placed at the pinnacle of the basilicas, on diadems, scepters, and coins. The alleged discovery of the wood of the Jerusalem cross and the worship rendered to it shows how the previous embarrassment transformed into devotion.

Yet the apparent incompatibility of divinity and crucifixion remained in paintings in a subtle way. In one of the best preserved paintings of the mid-seventh century, in the church of St. Maria Antica in Rome (see figure 1),[15] Jesus is shown with his eyes open and wearing a long robe, the colobium, to cover his body. (Convicts usually were stripped naked before crucifixion.) The Virgin Mary and John are on either side, and behind there are two soldiers. Christ's body stands on the cross with no clear means of support and so assumes the shape of a cross. The palms of his hands are open and relaxed, and the feet are close to each other and almost dangling but not crossed. With his eyes Jesus looks to his right side, where his mother stands, but he doesn't see her and seems to be looking somewhere beyond. This representation seems to avoid the suffering of the cross in favor of the

Figure 1

contemplation of God's sublimity and his victory over the powers of evil and death. With his hands opened, Jesus seems to hold the cosmos in a serene and protective embrace. The divinity and humanity of Jesus are transfigured into a presence that goes beyond the substance of this world and the weight of its mortality.

In a fragmentary icon of the seventh century preserved in the monastery of St. Catherine, Mount Sinai (see figure 2),[16] we can see the same sort of transcendence in Christ's posture. The body still covered by the long colobium, but this time the eyes are closed and the feet are well placed on a pedestal. The scene is enriched by the Virgin Mary and the apostle John, two or three soldiers drawing lots, one of the two thieves and, on top, the angels–a crowded representation of good and evil, human and divine, high and low. The closed eyes seem to show that the church had accepted the idea of a suffering and dead God. But there seems to be some embarrassment in showing the nakedness of Jesus, which perhaps shows some remaining problems with seeing something divine in the full human body.

In the Western world, we still do not know how to put body and spirit together, always considering one to be important and the other insignificant. This perspective is exactly opposite to the Eastern concept, as explained by Jung in his description of a pagoda during his travel in India:

> The pagoda is covered from base to pinnacle with exquisitely obscene sculptures. We talked for a long time about this extraordinary fact, which he explained to me as a means to achieve spiritualization. I objected–pointing to a group of young peasants who were standing open-mouthed before the monuments, admiring these splendors–that such young men were scarcely undergoing spiritualization at the moment, but were much more likely having their heads filled with sexual fantasies. Whereupon he replied, "But that is just the point. How can they ever become spiritualized if they do not first fulfill their karma? These admittedly obscene images are here for the very purpose of recalling to the people their dharma [law]; otherwise these unconscious fellows might forget it."[17]

Figure 2

We're not suggesting that your church bulletin should run a swimsuit issue, but it is nonetheless true that both body and spirit are vehicles of consciousness, and what we might consider inferior is also essential if we are to be whole. We are body and we are spirit at the same time, and denying one for the benefit of the other is simply a way of avoiding the human condition. If we accept the materialist's assumption that the spirit is not necessary, we end up living shallow and unconscious lives. If we accept the ascetic (and often New Age) denial of the body, we leave our spirits in a state of isolation, without the life, nourishment and means of expression by a healthy body provides.

The area of our body that has been most misinterpreted is the center: the genital and anal regions. This region, which embraces the great gifts of reproduction, creativity, and the elimination of waste, has been considered low, degrading, or vulgar for too long a time. It seems difficult for us to understand that the body is not antagonistic to the spirit, and that together they can lead us to a higher level of consciousness. Transcending the body implies that we must first be in the body–the reality of the body plays an essential role in the affirmation of the reality of the spirit. We need to learn how to live our spiritual side with ardor, intensity, and devotion–that is with physical vitality–while recognizing the essential need of keeping alive the priest, the mystic, within us.

There are two interesting images of the cross from Strasbourg that have a similar symbolism. The first represents Jesus hanging on a tree enriched with flowers and fruits (see figure 3);[18] the second, a bas relief of 1280, represents the cross as growing from Adam's grave (see figure 4).[19]

The tree used as a cross reminds us of Adam and the tree of knowledge of good and evil. This tree is commonly associated with the tree from which Jesus's cross is built. In this symbolism, the tree of knowledge is assimilated and transformed into an instrument of redemption. There is also a legend that Adam, the first man, was buried on the mountain of Golgotha, and so the cross planted on his grave means that a new humanity lies on the ashes of the old one, as a

Figure 3

Figure 4

redemption from the previous fall. In this sense, Jesus is considered the second Adam, the perfect achievement of all the potentialities of humankind. Again, we encounter the mysterious necessity for each one of us, to crucify a precious part of ourselves and, on the ashes of this passed reality, find the fruits of our salvation.

There is a beautiful and well-known cross in Florence by Giunta-Pisano (see figure 5),[20] that embellishes the cross with images and other ornaments, while showing the body of Christ in harmonic curves and with almost no visible wounds. This image signifies the artist's perception of the beauty and harmony of this experience when it is considered in its *glory*, rather than in its *tragedy*.

After the reformation, the image of Jesus on the cross seemed to become an exclusively Roman Catholic symbol, at least in the west. The Protestant churches developed a tendency to use the cross alone, to emphasize the risen Christ rather than the suffering one. This difference is also seen in the fact that, for Catholics, the Eucharist is a reenactment of that very holy moment on Good Friday; while for Protestants, the Eucharist is simply the celebration of a memory of that moment.

Still, both traditions emphasize the triumphant, glorious, transcendent Christ on the cross, whether or not they do so through images. For Protestants and Catholics alike, the cycle of crucifixion and resurrection are a dogma of faith, though this does not exclude any additional human attempt to understand it.

There is an eternal duality in all things, including suffering. Glory and salvation can arise if we accept the suffering that is the lot of all humanity and by doing so transform it into divine suffering. But if we do not understand this process of transformation, then the negative side of suffering may give rise to some form of masochism. This can be seen in the story of the young boy becoming a Lamed-Vov. The boy fantasizes grand self tortures until he learns the true nature of suffering and compassion.

All the basic forms of suffering are depicted in the crucifixion scenes. Mary and John experience natural suffering in watching Jesus die. The thieves on the left and right may be thought of as representing neurotic suffering. Christ in the center is undergoing the suffering in man necessary for both individuation and for opening the heart to compassion—transcendent suffering. The thief who becomes aware of this finds his suffering transformed. Mary as the suffering mother and observer symbolizes the natural suffering of life. The presence of the angels connects this entire experience to the transcendent, ensuring that it is a matter of soul.

As we build a better ego-Self relationship (our relationship with our own center and totality), we can penetrate the mystery of the cross more deeply. St. Augustine expressed this mystery beautifully, saying that Christ went to the cross like the bridegroom to the bride, with love, desire, humility, and responsibility. Such a wedding with suffering leads to a *vital* life at a higher level of consciousness, instead of remaining bogged down in an endless experience of pain.

Reynolds Price's entire book underscores this point and each case that we have presented points out the attainment of a richer, more satisfying life that is more open to truth, joy, and creativity. Whether we are healing neurotic pain, undergoing developmental suffering, or suffering from other natural causes, if we are on the path of individuation, toward transcendent suffering, we will find ourselves opened to the darkness of life as well as the light.

In ways small and large, suffering breaks through the limited personal context of our lives and opens us not only to passionate suffering, but to passionate joy; not only to fragmentation of our old selves, but also to passionate living that results in a deeper sense of completion.

The sophistication of modern life has lost its perspective on the mystery of the cross. This loss can be seen in Salvador Dali's painting "Crucifixion (Corpus Hypercubus)," (see figure 6).[21] The cross in Dali's painting has become a series of cubes suspended in the air. The hands and feet do not seem to be nailed, and there are no wounds, no blood. The central part of the body is blocked and contained within four cubes.

The face of Jesus is turned toward his upper right, and we do not see it. A richly dressed woman stands in the left corner on a ground lined with black and white tiles, which reproduce a shadow cross motif. A black sky fills the background with something like mountains on the horizon, giving more volume to the cross.

The light is mostly yellow, like the light of a strong artificial lamp. The picture appears more like a photograph than a painting, where nothing is left for the imagination. Every detail is perfectly reproduced and focused and yet the entire picture is fragmented and any notion of the blood and guts reality of such an act is absent.

If we compare this last painting with the first one, we can easily see how a *general idea of union* has been replaced by its opposite. The cubes which comprise the cross are not united but are simply close to each other as if they are held there by magnet fields. It seems that there are four cubes in a vertical row, then two on each side right and left, two front and back, and four other small cubes in front of Jesus.

The cubes are suspended above the ground, which is very good pictorial pun on the mathematical concept "raising to the third power (cubed)," and so shows the modern faith in human rationalism. The separation of the cubes also shows how modernism tries to give the illusion of wholeness with concepts and images that are mechanistic, fragmented, and ungrounded. This picture seems to be a better illustration of how man is crucified by modern life–how his soul is separated from his nature–than it is of the redemptive process of the story of Christ.

So if we look at the traditional cross in a symbolic way, we find that the foot of the cross is faith grounded in the deep foundation of the earth. The top is hope ascending upward to the sky. The width of the cross, the love that reaches even the enemies. So faith, hope, and love are gradually realized through reflection, suffering, and the wisdom of experience. And if Dali's painting is any indication, modern man, with his tendency toward concretism, abstraction, and rationalism, needs the faith, hope, and charity of the traditional cross now more than ever.

Figure 5

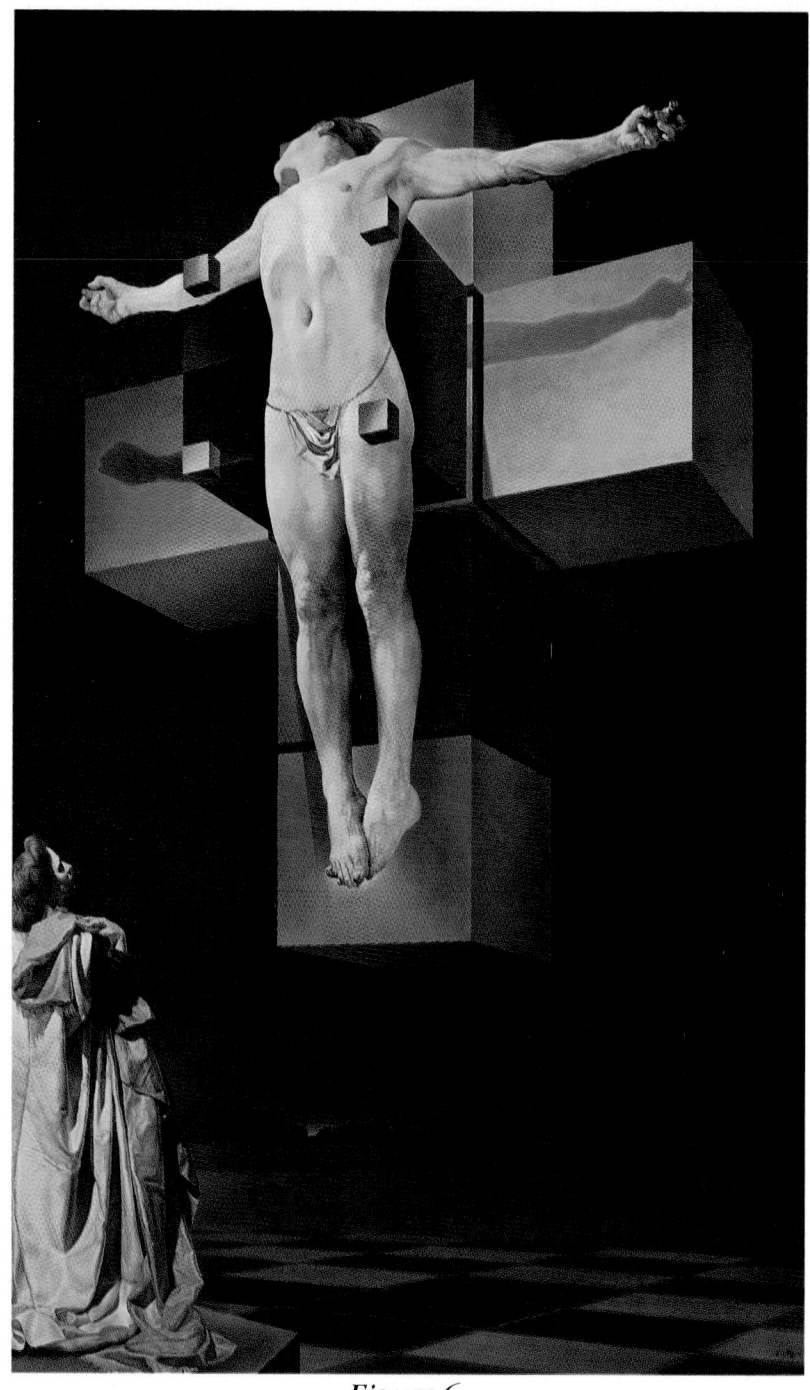

Figure 6

6

The Secret Initiation: Suffering as a Mystery

Our short, intense investigation of suffering through fairy tales, myths, and religions has shown us some important insights into the nature of suffering, insights that could lead to the healing of psychological wounds. But if we were to conclude at this point, the study would still be incomplete. There are further dimensions that we must consider.

There are some psychological wounds that never heal but remain open and always bleeding. There is no rational explanation for them and nothing can take away their torment. But while they may cause bitterness and destroy our capacity for life if we remain unconscious of them, these wounds can have meaning despite the fact that they are beyond our normal ability to heal. If we deal with these wounds consciously, they can develop into *sacred wounds* that may lead us to a particular destiny.

The meaning of our scared wounds is beyond our comprehension, but it is also absolutely present and tangible in our lives. This paradox of an accessible mystery can be found in the oldest shamanistic traditions and the secret nature of the ancient Greek Eleusinian Mysteries. The mystery should be maintained as a mystery and not subjected to shallow explanations. In the Eleusinian Mysteries, for instance, the heart of the ritual was considered too sacred to be put into words and therefore could never be divulged.[1] The ritual remained a true mystery in the profoundest religious sense of the term.

The Eleusinian Mysteries, the grandparents of the Western mystery religions and Western mysticism, gave us the complete ritual pattern for an initiation into a relationship with the Eternal. The Eternal is the great *unknown* that stands behind the many unknowns of our existence–birth, growth, aging, sexuality, spirituality, joy, suffering, and death. In the ancient world, rituals brought people into relationship with the *unknown* during the cycles of our lives to a greater or lesser extent. Both initiates and observers gained the feeling of being at one with themselves and existence as well as being bearers of the vital energy of life.

Mircea Eliade[2] pointed out that the value of suffering is clear in these early rituals. Even in primitive tribes the "suffering" in initiation ceremonies was required by superhuman beings in order to bring about the transmutation of the initiate through the expression of his or her death. This perspective is reflected in the Eleusinian mysteries through the dismembered god Dionysus and in the Christian tradition by Christ on the cross. Thus suffering is an "archetypal process" in the unification of spirit and nature, God and Man and in the spiritual transformation of humanity–coming into relationship with the *great unknowns.*

Mystics maintain that suffering is a necessary preparation for becoming open to transformation. Aristotle noted that the aim of initiation is not to learn, but to suffer. Even individuals undergoing fundamental changes in their personalities often dream of mythological motifs or suffering motifs. One man who was going through a significant life change involving a lot of inner suffering dreamed that a tribe of beautifully muscled African men were beating another group of equally splendid men and women with iron rods. The people being beaten were kneeling with arms outstretched in the shape of a cross, and bright red blood was dripping to the ground. These images suggest an intense inner (unconscious) suffering that may consciously be experienced as only a general feeling of oppression and uneasiness. Usually, more conscious suffering is not far away. Jung notes:

> "If the inner transformation enters more or less completely into consciousness, it becomes one of the most vivid and most decisive experiences a man can have of his individual fate."[3]

In the mystery rituals, sacred wounds are inflicted as part of the initiatory process. Life is also such a ritual, inflicting such wounds upon us. Whether we consciously understand their sacred nature or not determines whether we will participate in our destiny or simply become victims of our fate. Such wounds are often reflected metaphorically by the wedding of Persephone and Hades, and in ceremonies focused on purification such as sacrifices, prayers, fasting, and cleansing with water. To contemplate this metaphor, imagine the ceremony of closing your eyes and going inward, entering into the darkness, into the very beginning of life, where before creation there is only silence. Imagine understanding what the conscious mind cannot assimilate or explain, and keeping all of that inside and listening as Mary did in the gospel story: "As for Mary, she treasured all these things and pondered them in her heart" (Luke 2:19). In his discussion of why his new life was better for him, Reynolds Price pointed out that:

> ...paraplegia, with its maddening limitations has forced a degree of patience and consequent watchfulness on me. ... I heard two of Franklin Roosevelt's sons say that the primary change in their father, after polio struck him in mid-life and grounded him firmly, was an increased patience and a willingness to listen.[4]

A religious attitude toward these wounds engenders the silence that comes in loneliness and isolation, forcing us to look inward, hear the conflict, and the pulse of life and then reach for resources beyond our normal human capacity and understanding. In one form or another, this process leads to recognizing the *mystery* of the autonomous creativity of the unconscious as part of the creativity of the life process.

The meaning of natural suffering–the sorrowful course of human history, the cruelty of nature, and the blindness of providence and how to respond to it have always been central questions for humankind. Viktor Frankl enriched our understanding of suffering by reflecting on his own experiences in the concentration camps and how they directed him to become a physician to the soul. He pointed out that when we are faced by something unalterable, imposed by fate then:

> . . . the manner in which a person takes these things upon himself, assimilates these difficulties into his own psyche, there flows an incalculable multitude of value potentialities. This means that *human life can be fulfilled not only in creating and enjoying, but also in suffering!*[5]

He goes on to say that a cult of material success and happiness cannot come to grips with the depth of life. We need suffering to guard us from apathy, "psychic rigor-mortis," and to reveal the deep wisdom in our emotions, "superior to all reason, which in fact runs counter to the gospel of rationalistic utility."[6]

Our finest literature reflects the opening and deepening of the human heart in response to the suffering of life. Alessandro Manzoni, in his famous novel *The Betrothed*, simply and elegantly illustrates our theme. His story takes place in the city of Milan during the plague in the Middle Ages. Society has completely broken down, and the authorities have fled. The church fathers, except for a few heroic exceptions, have deserted their posts and closed their doors, and the most dreadful side of human nature had risen to the surface along with pestilence, death, and famine. In the midst of this living horror were the lowest of the low, the monatti, scavengers who collected the bodies of the dead, robbing them, their homes, and often their helpless and dependent families. Though they accepted bribes to bury the dead decently, they rarely fulfilled their promises and simply dumped the bodies outside the city.

In the midst of this abominable scene, a woman stepped out of a doorway toward the carts of the dead.

> She was young, though no longer in the first bloom of youth and there was still beauty in her face, a beauty veiled and dimmed but not destroyed by unbearable emotion and a deadly weakness . . . Her step was tired but firm; she shed no tears now, though she had clearly shed many before. There was something profound in her grief, which bore witness to a heart that felt its sorrows deeply and constantly.[7]

In her arms she bore the carefully dressed and prepared body of her little daughter. The loathsome monatto she approached showed clear respect, touched his hand to his heart, and promised not to bother the little body once the mother prepared her a place on the cart with her own hands. The monatti were solicitous and deferential and promised to "lay her in the earth exactly as she is."[8]

The mother kissed and blessed her child and asked the monatti to return tomorrow for her and her other daughter. Both had the mark of death on their faces as they watched the cart depart. Manzoni continues:

> . . . and what could she do then but lay her one remaining child on the bed, and lie down beside her so that they could die, together, as the flower already blossoming on its stem falls together with the bud beside it, as the passing of the scythe which lays low grass and flowers alike?
>
> 'Dear God, hear her prayer!' cried Renzo (the observer and a main character in the book).
>
> 'Take her to yourself, together with the little one!'[9]

Through this touching story Manzoni reveals that the human values of attention, love, respect, and dignity can transform the worst of horrors. In this scene, dignity that springs from the human soul draws respect and compassion from the worst in human nature, bringing about a state of Grace. Such Grace is the foundation of human life and when we experience it, we can find meaning and "a peace that passeth understanding," even in the face of the worst that life can offer.

Padre Pio of Pietrelcina, possibly the best known Christian mystic of this century, used the following folktale (a metaphor that I have also heard attributed to G.K. Chesterton) to illustrate how we have to shift our perspective in order to understand the mysterious relationship of suffering to life.

> There is a woman who is embroidering. Her son seated on a low stool, sees her work, but in reverse. He sees the knots of the embroidery, the tangled threads . . . He says, 'Mother, what are you doing? I can't make out what you are doing!' Then the mother lowers the embroidery hoop and shows the good part of the work. Each color is in place and the various threads form a harmonious design. So, we see the reverse side of the embroidery because we are seated on too low a stool.[10]

These mysteries and our response to them turns life itself into an initiation process for each of us, bringing us into the wholeness of living and communion with the eternal. If we can understand this and participate in it, life will transform us. It is in this sense that Jung determined that man is "indispensable for the completion of creation . . . accepting the inscrutable design that reveals itself and never trying to push through his own way . . ."[11]

We no longer seem to be able to answer the question, "Why is this happening to me?" As we have lost our capacity to deal with mystery, we have also lost sight of the deeper reality that supports life and with it our ability to deal with the deeper pains of life. Even in the throes of loneliness and despair, we are taught to suppress our feelings, conceal our pain, and present a happy face to the world. No more cries for help and comfort. No more sackcloth and ashes, beating our breasts, tearing our hair and weeping. The only ways we know how to respond to painful situations are to fight back against them or ignore them, either one of which leaves us at war with ourselves and nature–eternally torn asunder.

Mourning is one of the greatest healers of our developmental wounds, and without it we can never fully open the door to our own creativity, not to mention our own humanity. Without mourning, our encounters with the major events of life are turned into neurotic pain that blocks our living energy. When we take an aggressive or self-deceptive approach to suffering, we deaden ourselves to life. As we suppress the old laments, they frequently return under the disguise of autism, depression, and addiction. The meaning of suffering has been misplaced, and we are often left lost and helpless, with only the pathology of our children before us.

Sacred wounds bring us to choices. These are choices that we must make each time we face one of the great unknowns. The pearl, centuries-old symbol of the incorruptible product of a life's work, often forms from the grit of suffering. If we are open and respond to it, suffering brings us into our own full humanity and our full awareness of the divine in us. It leads us to create a soul, our pearl, where the two contrary forces of flesh and spirit can become fellow workers rather than enemies.

7

Opening the Heart— Tempering the Soul: Conclusion

We began our reflection by taking a look at the word "suffering," and from there looked at its content. We described four different forms of suffering: natural, developmental, neurotic, and transcendent. Then throughout this book, we have briefly touched on topics that could fill books of their own. We hope you will use our discussions as cornerstones for your own reflection, building on them as your own psyche suggests.

Suffering, however neurotic, psychotic, or more or less normal it may be, reflects our fundamental human experience. Throughout the centuries the reality of suffering has been concealed, displaced, avoided, denied, and/or projected–as we saw when we compared the two versions of Cinderella. But the way the theme of suffering keeps reappearing in stories, fairy tales, myths, and religions shows the archetypal nature of suffering and its importance to our lives.

Suffering is a necessary step in increasing awareness and in the development of our personality, as the myth of Inanna shows. This myth portrays the deep inner journey of the development of the feminine in the psyche. Feminine consciousness, which Jung also described as "lunar consciousness" after the mild light of the moon that merges things together rather than separating them, is indeed torturous to develop in the practical world.

In contrast to the myth of Inanna, the story of Prometheus suggests a more extroverted manner of suffering. Prometheus portrays the development of masculine consciousness, or what Jung called "solar consciousness," for the sun in whose bright light everything can be seen and discriminated. In both myths, we see the ardor and the passion that marks these two different journeys, both components of the greater journey we call individuation.

C.S. Lewis's story of the angel and the ghost illustrates the process of transformation. This story described the fear and the suffering that our ego goes through when transformed by the Self. The above story shows that neurotic pain arises when our own vital processes are blocked. The purpose of analysis in such a case is often not to heal the pain, but to make the conflict understandable and bring it into consciousness. The neurotic pain is transformed into true suffering, and our own life process can then go on. Life must be continually faced and known in this way in order to be vitally lived. This is why Jungians generally use the term "transformation," rather than "healing," when dealing with psychic pain.

Our brief overview of religious perspectives on suffering looked at specific contributions from three different traditions. With their symbols of salvation, they could be considered different forms of psychotherapy–different ways to deal with the suffering of the soul. Each, in its own way, also connects suffering to the eternal and the transcendent. The Buddhist and Yoga philosophies, on the other hand, showed an original approach to the suffering of both the soul and the body. The Yoga tradition considers pain to be positive because it reminds us to withdraw from the world in order to realize the true nature of spirit. In Buddhism, suffering also acquires a positive value, as it is the primary way to pay our karmic debt, which determines our future existence.

The story of Christ gave us the opportunity to study the gospels from a psychological perspective. We included only a few details of Christ's life and parables, just enough to illustrate how ego development in the second half of life is a parallel to the Christian message.

Finally we looked at the mysterious aspects of suffering, recognizing that human understanding of the whole of suffering must paradoxically contain elements beyond our comprehension.

Suffering brings us into touch with the great unknowns at every stage of our psychological development as well as those in every fateful event in life. These unknowns are forces that may drive us beyond where we planned to go, and even threaten our ego's existence. But by accepting the mysteries, participating in them, we are able to become at home in a dreadful world and discover the deeper pulse of life.

To be an initiated one in the mysteries of life changes our consciousness and our relationship to ourselves, the world, and God. As we go through our individuation process and our suffering transforms from developmental or neurotic into transcendent, we find that more and more it is the divine aspect in us that suffers. We reclaim our capacity to consciously carry our wounds and open ourselves to the ambiguities, the conflicts, and the contradictions of the human condition. Suffering and acting become a dialectic, and the wounds of life open us to the process of becoming in which joy follows as naturally as Easter follows Good Friday in the Christian story. Joy is also a mystery which paradoxically cannot be achieved. It can only be attained through an openness to participating in life.

When we are able to carry our own wounds and even wound someone else in the service of life, we become able to serve purpose that the life within us, the Self, is asking us to serve. We become transformative agents in the greater story of culture. As such we can, perhaps, help keep others from suffering for the wrong reasons and surely join others in the human experience with true compassion. We also find that our lives transform from the plodding work of existence to a sacred task and finally to a sacred mission.

In dealing with suffering, analysts to some extent share the same professional field as psychologists and doctors. However, our approach differs in that we not only study the theories of psychology, but also experience their validity within our own personal lives as we train. Medical doctors, in general, try to label symptoms and then apply the proper treatment. Analysts prove their process in their own inner work and then share in the transformative process of analysis along with the analysand. As Jung wrote:

> It should be clear from the foregoing discussion that everything psychotherapy has in common with symptomatology

> clinically understood–i.e. with the medical picture–is, I will not say irrelevant, but of secondary importance in so far as the medical picture of disease is a provisional one. The real and important thing is the psychological picture, which can only be discovered in the course of treatment behind the veil of pathological symptoms.[1]

The goal of medicine and mainstream psychology is to relieve the pain, and health consists of a return to "normal" or the previous status quo. The goal of Jungian psychology is often to deepen and amplify the pain until the meaning of it becomes clear. The meaning helps us find the purpose of our suffering and directs us toward a reorganization of life on a higher (or deeper) and more authentic level.

When we allow the autonomous creativity of our own nature to come to life, suffering becomes a personal and cultural stimulus to growth. Suffering is then the creative energy of humankind. Suffering as a human condition can never be understood by simply thinking about it. Such a view ignores the power of emotions. Neither can simply feeling our suffering give us a complete picture of the process. We need to analyze the different stages of psychological development and transformation in order to have a more lucid understanding of the aspects of suffering. But we must also remain aware of the fact that by doing so, we run the risk of destroying the meaning of suffering. The importance of suffering will always be that it drives us toward wholeness, toward reaching the totality of the psyche, in the context of the mystery of the full experience of life. Understanding and accepting the vitality and the necessity of suffering is an agonizing, difficult task, a task that rouses our souls.

We must learn not to be afraid. We can gain new, creative, and unexpected perspectives from our suffering. We can learn that in the tears of suffering, we can find the salt of wisdom, the heart of life, and an opening to the experience of passionate joy.

Epilogue

. . . often a hand hovered before me in the air, a hand with an eternally renewed wound: someone seemed to have driven a nail through it, seemed to be driving a nail through it for all eternity.

–Niko Kazantzakis
Saint Francis

May God deny you peace, but give you glory.

–Unamuno
The Tragic Sense of Life

Notes

(Full bibliographical details appear in the **Bibliography**.)

Abbreviation: C.W. = C.G. Jung. 1959. *The Collected Works.* Translated by R. F. C. Hull, edited by H. Read, M. Fordham, G. Adler, William McGuire. Bollingen Series XX, Vols. 1–20 (Princeton: Princeton University Press and London: Routledge and Kegan Paul), paragraph numbers.

1 FOREWORD: PAIN, SUFFERING, TRANSFORMATION, AND JOY

[1]Helen Luke, *The Voice Within*, p. 89.

[2]G. Jobes, *Dictionary of Mythology and Symbols.*

[3]Evelyn Underhill, *Practical Mysticism*, p. 27.

[4]C.G. Jung, C.W., Vol. 16, 185.

[5]Projection is the psychological term for the unconscious displacement of our personal attributes onto other people or objects. The projected contents may be unacceptable emotions or qualities or they may be beneficial and valuable. The recollection and integration of projected contents is an important part of Jungian analysis and any journey into self-understanding.

[6]American Heritage Dictionary, (1983) Dell Publishing Company.

[7]The individuation process is the process of self-development in which a person matures and becomes

increasingly conscious of their psychological aspects and continually integrates them into a unique personality that is individual and is evolving its own meaningful pattern of living.

[8]C.S. Lewis, *The Great Divorce*, pp. 98–103.

[9]C.G. Jung, C.W., Vol. 17, 154.

[10]A.W. Frank, *What Kind of Phoenix? Illness and Self-Knowledge*, pp. 39, 40.

[11]Laurens van der Post eloquently discussed moaning music, friendship with pain, and compassion in his chapter "The Greater Uprooter" in *About Blady: A Pattern Out of Time.*

2 THE SEARCH FOR OURSELVES: AN ILLUSTRATION OF SUFFERING IN A FAIRY TALE

[1]C.G. Jung, C.W., Vol. 8, 109.

[2]Grimm Brothers, *The Complete Fairy Tales.*

[3]H. Schecter & J.G. Semeiks, *Patterns in Popular Culture*, pp. 168–72.

[4]C. G. Jung postulated that each person has an opposite sex component in their psychological personality. He termed the feminine aspect in a man the anima and the masculine aspect in a woman the animus. The emotional effects of the opposite sex parent is the primary formational influence on this part of one's personality.

[5]Fritz Zorn, *Mars*, p. 54.

[6]Ibid, p. 72.

[7]Ibid, pp. 117–18.

[8]Reynolds Price, *A Whole New Life*, p. 183.

3 THE FABRIC OF OUR LIVES: SUFFERING IN MYTHOLOGY

[1]Joseph Campbell, *The Power of Myth*, p. 91.

[2]Diane Wolkstein & Samuel Noah Kramer, *Inanna Queen of Heaven and Earth,* p. 52.

[3]Dante, *The Inferno*, Canto III, lines 1–9.

[4]Ibid, lines 9–15.

[5]Ibid, line 16.

[6]C.G. Jung, *Memories, Dreams and Reflections*, p. 189.
[7]Ibid, pp. 184–85.
[8]A. Van Gennep, *The Rites of Passage.*
[9]M. Esther Harding, *Psychic Energy*, Chapter 3.
[10]M. P. O. Marford & R. J. Lenardon, *Classical Mythology*, pp. 235–36.
[11]C.G. Jung, *C. G. Jung Letters*, Vol. 11, pp. 492–93.
[12]Diane Wolkstein & Samuel Noah Kramer, *Inanna Queen of Heaven and Earth*, p. 4.
[13]M. Esther Harding, *Psychic Energy*, p. 57.
[14]Hesiod, *Theogony Works and Days.*
[15]G. Murray, *The Complete Plays of Aeschylus.*
[16]Ibid.
[17]C.G. Jung, C.W., Vol. 9ii, 203.
[18]C.G. Jung, C.W., Vol .7, 243 note.
[19]J.E. Cirlot, *Dictionary of Symbols.*

4 FIRE AND EMPTINESS: A BRIEF PERSPECTIVE ON SUFFERING IN RELIGIONS

[1]C.G. Jung, C.W. Vol. 11, 734.
[2]C.G. Jung, *C.G. Jung Letters*, Vol. 1, p. 236.
[3]M. Eliade, *The Encyclopedia of Religion*, p. 100.
[4]Sheldon Kopp (1972), *If You Meet the Buddha on the Road, Kill Him*, pp. 15-16.
[5]Ibid, p. 15.
[6]Ibid, p. 16.
[7]M. Eliade, *The Encyclopedia of Religion*, p. 102.
[8]C.G. Jung, *Man and His Symbol*, p. 82.

5 THE COSMIC PILGRIMAGE: JESUS CHRIST AND THE CROSS ILLUSTRATE TRANSFORMATION THROUGH TIME

[1]C.G. Jung, C.W. Vol. 11, 734.
[2]C.G. Jung, *C.G. Jung Letters*, Vol. 1, p. 236.
[3]M. Eliade, *The Encyclopedia of Religion*, p. 100.
[4]Joseph Campbell, *The Power of Myth*, p. 112.
[5]Edward Edinger, *Ego and Archetype*, p. 136.
[6]Ibid.
[7]Sam Keen, *Voices and Visions*, interview with Joseph

Campbell, p. 79.
[8]Paul J. Achtemeier, gen. ed., *Harpers Bible Dictionary*, pp. 640–41.
[9]C.G. Jung, C.W., Vol. 9ii, 8.
[10]Ibid, Vol. 10, 449.
[11]Leonard Boff, *Passion of Christ, Passion of the World.*
[12]Evelyn Underhill, *Mysticism.*
[13]C.G. Jung, C.W., Vol. 11, 415.
[14]Ibid, Vol. 11, 427–28.
[15]D. T. Rice, *A Concise History of Painting From Prehistory to the Thirteenth Century.*
[16]Ibid.
[17]C.G. Jung, *Memories, Dreams and Reflections*, p. 277.
[18]C.G. Jung, C.W., Vol. 5, p. xxxvi.
[19]Ibid, p. xxxvii.
[20]H. L. C. Jaffe, *The History of World Painting.*
[21]R. Descharnes, *Dali.*

6 THE SECRET INITIATIONS: SUFFERING AS A MYSTERY

[1]C. Kerény, "The Mysteries of the Kabeiroi," p. 38.
[2]M. Eliade, "Mystery and Spiritual Regeneration in Extra-European Religions," p. 17.
[3]C.G. Jung, "Transformation Symbolism in the Mass," p. 336.
[4]Reynolds Price, *A Whole New Life,* pp. 18906.
[5]Viktor Frankl, *The Doctor and the Soul*, pp. 105–106.
[6]Ibid, p. 118.
[7]Alessandro Manzoni, *The Betrothed*, pp. 639–40.
[8]Ibid.
[9]Ibid.
[10]C. C. Benard Ruffin, *Padre Pio: The True Story*, p. 143.
[11]Barbara Hannah, *Jung: His Life and Work*, p. 173.

7 OPENING THE HEART–TEMPERING THE SOUL: CONCLUSION

[1]C.G. Jung, C.W., Vol. 16, 210.

Bibliography

Achtemeier, P.J., gen. ed. 1985. *Harper's Bible Dictionary.* San Francisco: Harper & Row.

Boff, Leonard. 1987. *Passion of Christ, Passion of the World.* New York: Orbis.

Bryant, C. 1978. *The River Within: The Search for God in Depth.* London: Darton, Longman & Todd.

Campbell, J. 1988. *The Power of Myth.* With Bill Moyers. New York: Doubleday.

Cirlot, J.E. 1987. *A Dictionary of Symbols.* New York: Philosophical Library.

Dante, A. 1982. *The Divine Comedy, Inferno.* Translated by A. Mandelbaum. New York: Bantam.

Descharnes, R. 1985. *Dali.* Translated by E.R. Morse. New York: Harry N. Abrams.

Edinger, E. 1972. *Ego and Archetype.* New York: Penguin Book.

Eliade, M. 1987. *The Encyclopedia of Religion.* New York: Macmillan Publishing.

Eliade, M. 1964. "Mystery and Spiritual Regeneration in Extra-European Religions." In *Man and Transformation,* edited by J. Campbell. Bollingen Series XXX5. Princeton: Princeton/Bollingen.

Frank, A.W. 1992. "What Kind of Phoenix? Illness and Self Knowledge." *Second Opinion* (October): 31, 41.

Frankl, V.E. 1973. *The Doctor and the Soul.* Translated by R. & C. Winston. New York: Vintage.

Grimm Brothers. 1972. *The Complete Grimm's Fairy Tales.* New York: Pantheon Books.

Harding, E. 1973. *Psychic Energy.* New York: Princeton University Press, Bollingen Foundation.

Hesiod. 1988. *Theogony Works and Days.* Translated by M.L. West. New York: Oxford University Press.

Jaffe, H.L.C. (ed.) 1966. *The History of World Painting.* New York: Alpine.

Jobes, G. *Dictionary of Mythology, Folklore and Symbols.*

The Scarecrow Press.

Jung, C.G. *The Collected Works.* Translated by R.F.C. Hull, edited by H. Read, M. Fordham, G. Adler, William. McGuire. Bollingen Series XX, Vols. 1–20. Princeton: Princeton University Press, and London: Routledge and Kegan Paul.

Jung, C.G. 1976. *C.G. Jung Letters.* Vol. 1 and II. London: Routledge & Kegan.

Jung, C.G. (conceived and ed.) 1964. *Man and His Symbols.* New York: Doubleday.

Jung, C.G. 1973. *Memories, Dreams and Reflections.* New

York: Pantheon.

Jung, C. G. 1955. "Transformation Symbolism in the Mass." In *Man and Transformation.* Edited by J. Campbell. Bollingen Series XXX2. Princeton: Princeton/Bollingen.

Keen, S. 1974. *Voices and Visions: Talks with Sam Keen.* New York: Harper & Row.

Kerény, C. 1955. "The Mysteries of the Kabeiroi." In *The Mysteries.* Edited by J. Campbell. Bollingen Series XXX2. Princeton: Princeton/Bollingen.

Kopp, S.B. 1972. *If You Meet the Buddha on the Road, Kill Him.* California: Science and Behavior.

Kung, H. 1987. *Christianity and the World Religions.* London: Collins.

Lewis, C.S. 1946. *The Great Divorce.* New York: Macmillan Publishing Co.

Luke, H. 1988. *The Voice Within: Love and Virtue in the Age of Spirit.* New York: Crossroad.

Manzoni, A. 1972. *The Betrothed.* Translated by B. Penman. England: Penguin.

Marford, M. P. O. & Lenardon, R. J. 1985. *Classical Mythology.* New York: Longman.

Murray, G. 1952. *The Complete Plays of Aeschylus.* London: George Allen & Unwin Ltd.

Price, R. 1994. *A Whole New Life.* New York: Antheneum.

Rice, D.T. 1967. *A Concise History of Painting From Prehistory to the Twentieth Century.* New York: Frederick A. Praeger.

Ruffin, C.B. 1991. *Padre Pio: The True Story.* Huntington, Indiana: Sunday Visitor Publishing.

Schechter, H. & Semeiks, J.G. 1980. *Patterns in Popular Culture.* New York: Harper & Row.

The Thompson Chain-Reference Bible. 1983. New York.

Underhill, E. 1974. *Mysticism.* New York: Meridian Books.

Underhill, E. 1942. *Practical Mysticism.* Columbus, Ohio: Ariel.

Wolkstein, D. and Kramer, S.N. 1983. *Inanna Queen of Heaven and Earth.* New York: Harper & Row.

Zorn, F. 1982. *Mars.* New York: Alfred A. Knopf.

Index

Books By C.T.B. Harris, Ph.D.

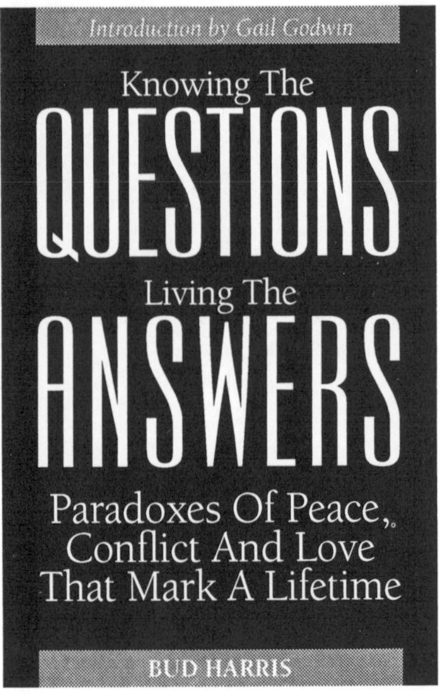

A book about learning to hear and interpret the nudgings and messages from our "inner blueprint", which Harris defines as "the pattern of creation longing to be fulfilled within each of us." The more conscious we become of our personal pattern, the better we will be able to *live* the answers to life's questions, rather than suffering through them.

"Accessible and satisfying. We immediately trust Dr. Harris as he reflects on…life."

Gail Godwin
Author

AVAILABLE AT BETTER BOOKSTORES

Or from Northstar Publications. Publication date: Fall 1996